Indians As Mascots

In

Minnesota Schools

by

Pat Helmberger

Friends of the Bill of Rights Foundation
Burnsville, Minnesota

LIBRARY OF CONGRESS CATALOG CARD NUMBER:
99-714199

ISBN: 0-9668828-0-6

PRINTED AND BOUND IN
THE UNITED STATES OF AMERICA

Published by:
FRIENDS OF THE BILL OF RIGHTS FOUNDATION
107 Professional Plaza
1601 East Highway 13
Burnsville, Minnesota 55337

December, 1999

INTRODUCTION

Friends of the Bill of Rights Foundation is delighted with this opportunity to publish and freely distribute INDIANS AS MASCOTS IN MINNESOTA SCHOOLS. Ms Pat helmberger, the distinguished author, has written, as a labor of love, the second book in what we hope will be a continuing series of works on important social issues. Matthew Stark, now the executive director emeritus of the Minnesota Civil Liberties Union, deserves our thanks for his leadership as executive director and then president of the MCLU in regard to the issue of the depiction of American Indians as mascots in Minnesota schools and the need to treat the First Americans as first class citizens.

Matt, and Clyde Bellecourt, one of the founders of the American Indian Movement, had earlier worked together on several civil liberties issues involving American Indians and Matt was therefore able to secure assistance and leadership from Clyde and his colleagues. Also, Matt and Dr. Clara Sue Kidwell, and her family had been friends for years, and he was able to call upon her and her network of national Indian leaders for guidance and support.

In the early 1980s, Matt had been successful in securing funding from the Northwest Area Foundation of which Ms Terry Sarrio was then president and from the Otto Bremer Foundation of which John Kostishack was and is the executive director for the hiring of law student interns at the Minnesota Civil Liberties Union Foundation. Therefore, fortunately, Susan Aasen was on the staff of the MCLUF as a law student intern when the issue written about in this book arose. This history tells of her significant role leading to success.

Willie Hardacker was also involved with the MCLUF as a law student intern and was therefore also available to go to reservation areas in northern Minnesota to search for clients. Our sincere thanks go to these two lawyers for their fine work. Also, of course, the boards of directors of these two civic minded foundations deserve our thanks.

Robert J. Bruno, Esq. President
FRIENDS OF THE BILL OF RIGHTS FOUNDATION
November 1999

ACKNOWLEDGMENTS

Writing the Indian mascot history has been, without question, the most fascinating project on which I have ever embarked. I began with some hesitation, however, because I cannot speak as an American Indian. I am a non-Indian and I make no claim to fully understand the long painful history that my friends, who are American Indians, share as their legacy. I am grateful to them for their kind patience in helping me through some of the insecurities I felt as I worked on this project.

It follows then, that my friend Phil St. John of the Sisseton Wahpeton Dakota Nation, receives my gratitude for his advice and knowledge, not only about historical events, but in the proper identification of American Indian people. He has assured me that either "American Indian" or "Indian" is proper usage although many American Indians prefer to be identified by tribe or nation. I have attempted to follow those guidelines except in quotations where the speaker uses terms such as "Native American" or simply "native."

I began compiling background material for this book six years ago. Having been part of the movement to eliminate Indian mascots, I knew this was an historic effort. Minnesota was indeed the first state to address this issue in its public schools. Through a chance conversation with Dr. Matthew Stark, then executive director emeritus of the Minnesota Civil Liberties Union, I mentioned the work I was doing to record this important Minnesota movement. He immediately expressed interest in my work and offered to help make available to me the voluminous material on file at the MCLU office concerning the issue of Indians as mascots in Minnesota public high schools. Because the MCLU had played a vital role in the mascot issue, it seemed like a natural match.

Since that day, he has become my steadfast compatriot in my writing of this history. With his English teacher's training and his determination to make this an important historical document, he spared no red pencil in his editing and left no stone unturned in helping to put this puzzle together. As a scholar, he delighted in locating people we wanted to interview and in gleaning historical facts from long-archived committee meetings. Because of it, I believe this book is both historically accurate and easily readable, goals to which both of us aspired. We want students, teachers, school administrators, professional and college teams, sports enthusiasts, and the general public, to hear the message of change. I owe Matt a deep debt of gratitude for all he has done to help me in the recounting of this fascinating bit of history.

In the course of my work, I have met and interviewed many people and have been assisted by many others. Each has been gracious and each has added a wider dimension to my knowledge. My deep appreciation goes to: Susan Aasen, Paul Sand, Dr. Will Antell, Lucinda Jesson, Debbie Mancheski, Professor Clara Sue Kidwell, Suzan Shown Harjo, Jodi Cramsie, Clyde Bellecourt, Fred Veilleux, Ruth Meyers, Yvonne Novak, Marsha Gronseth, Pat Tupper, Ted Suss, Steve Brenhaug, the Minnesota Civil Liberties Union, the Minnesota Indian Education Division of the Minnesota Department of Education, and the Michigan Civil Rights Department.

I have woven many events and many voices into this story of conflict, courage, and change. Thanks to all of you who have graciously provided the threads.

Pat Helmberger
November 1999
Bloomington, MN

FOREWORD

In popular wisdom, high school athletics programs instill in students a sense of sportsmanship, teamwork, and good citizenship. They also, however, foster intense competitiveness. High school, college, and professional teams choose mascots that represent strength and cunning - predatory animals such as eagles, panthers, and bears. Some select Indians or warriors, sometimes with the ostensible intent of honoring American Indian people, and sometimes to adopt images of savagery and violence that fit the values of competition and victory.

The mascot is a double-edged sword. To the team that uses it, it represents winning qualities, but to the opposing team, it represents the enemy. In the world of competitive sports, part of the game is disparaging the enemy. Indians are there to be scalped, tomahawked, burned at the stake, killed, or at the very least, to be ridiculed and humiliated in any number of creative ways. When winning means not how the game is played but upholding the honor of the school, sports take on characteristics of warfare, an experience all too common in the past history of American Indian tribes.

The use of American Indians as mascots for sports teams has sparked intense emotions - resentment and anger from Indian people who feel that they are being caricatured, ridiculed, and shamed; resentment and scorn from students, parents, school administrators, and the non-Indian public who feel that their motives are misunderstood, or who don't understand what the protests are all about. As some of the first organizations in the nation to examine the use of Indians as sports mascots in public schools, the Concerned American Indian Parents in Minneapolis, Minnesota, and the Minnesota Civil Liberties Union have helped to focus attention on the issues raised by these mascots.

One issue is, who speaks for Indians? Indians have become accustomed but not resigned to the appropriation of their identity in the form of mascots, advertising symbols, movie Indians - stereotypical images that convey a sense of savagery and inferiority. The generalized image of the Plains warrior in feather bonnet and loincloth adorns the halls of schools throughout the nation. One school with an Indian identity, however, is the high school in the Red Lake reservation in Northern Minnesota. The school's enrollment is 100% Ojibwe, and its basketball team is the Warriors - a name used with pride by students and the Red Lake community. Here the Warriors are real Indians. The Warriors allow students and the community to speak for themselves. The hurt in the use of Indian mascots by non-Indian teams is the stereotypes that these teams adopt. Schools cannot speak for Indian people. They can only act out the images that they have seen in movies, advertising, and television.

A second issue is that mascots dehumanize real people by perpetrating stereotypical and derogatory images of American Indians. In the process they both focus on social and economic problems in Indian communities - high rates of alcoholism, poverty, and unemployment - and dull public sensibility to positive steps that tribes are taking to strengthen their integrity and stability. While the Congress of the United States considers legislation to destroy the sovereignty of tribal governments, diminishing tax advantages that allow them to attract business development to create jobs, fans of the Atlanta Braves do the Tomahawk chop and celebrate their caricatured image of an Indian warrior.

The third issue is how the mascot preempts the history of American Indians in school curricula. The mascot is highly visible and receives major attention on the sports field or court, while in textbooks Indians generally rate a few pages in an introductory chapter on the Americas before European discovery and then largely disappear from the historical record. Where they to appear is in accounts of the Trail of Tears - the forcible removal of the Cherokees from their homelands in North Carolina, Georgia and Tennessee to the Indian Territory (now the state of Oklahoma) west of the Mississippi River, or the Battle of the Little Big Horn where George Armstrong Custer and his men died in a futile attack on a Sioux camp, or the massacre of some 300 Lakota people at Wounded Knee Creek in South Dakota in 1890.

Indian mascots perpetrate the image that Indians are people of the past. They often play on stereotypes of savagery, drunkenness, and backwardness. They deny the voices of Indian people who want to portray themselves as proud and sovereign people living in contemporary America, surviving and even flourishing as self-sufficient communities. They simplify very complex issues of how people view themselves and how others view them. And despite the emotions that surround their use, they can be used to explore the issues of cultural identity and cultural communication.

The value of this book is that it explores those issues. No one who reads it carefully can fall back on simplistic statements such as, "We want to honor Indians", or "We can't be responsible for what our parents or grandparents or great-grandparents did," or even, "We are being victimized by an oppressive society". The hope is that dialogue between Indian and non-Indian people about the emotional dimensions of the issues will lead to greater understanding in the future.

Dr. Clara Sue Kidwell, Director
Native America Studies Program
University of Oklahoma

AUTHOR'S NOTES

This book is a history of three groups' involvement in the American Indian mascot issue. Those groups are The Minnesota Civil Liberties Union, the Concerned American Indian Parents, and the National Conference of Christians and Jews, Minnesota Dakotas Region. Each believes that the use of American Indian names and images as mascots and team names hurts Indian people, especially children who often feel embarrassed by the antics of "make believe" Indians on the gym floor or on the sports field. Each was determined to end that practice.

The Minnesota Civil Liberties Union (MCLU), established in 1952, is famous for protecting freedom of speech and separation of church and state. Its controversial stands have placed it in the cross-fires of public opinion on many occasions and the Indian mascot issue was no exception. The MCLU viewed it within the framework of the Equal Protection Clause of the Fourteenth Amendment of the U. S. Constitution rather than as a free speech issue and that raised the eyebrows of some civil libertarians. Dr. Matthew Stark was the executive director of the MCLU when this issue surfaced in 1986. He saw to it then, and since, that the MCLU gave this issue its serious attention, support, and leadership. The second group, Concerned American Indian Parents (CAIP), was formed in 1987 by Phil St. John, a member of the Sisseton Wahpeton Dakota Nation, and a chemical dependency counselor who lives and works in Minneapolis. For years he had been angered by the misuse of Indian images. When his own children hung their heads in shame while watching a white Minneapolis Southwest high school student dressed in feathers and war paint, whooping and screaming, he knew it was time to do something about it. He spoke with other Indian people who shared his resolve for change and together they formed the CAIP.

The third group is the Minnesota Dakotas Region of the National Conference of Christians and Jews, headquartered in Minneapolis. It is an organization dedicated to religious understanding and human rights and usually works quietly within the community. Its director, Paul Sand, had worked with the United Sioux tribes in South Dakota, looking for ways to help tribal governments bring employment to their isolated areas. He had also led and participated in a human rights conference in Sioux Falls, South Dakota, where Indian people testified before members of Congress about discrimination that takes place daily in every aspect of their lives:

banking, medical emergency care, education, restaurant service, and employment. I served as administrative assistant to Mr. Sand and both of us were members of the MCLU board of directors when the Indian mascot issue surfaced as a civil rights complaint. Later, after reading an article in the *Star Tribune* newspaper about St. John's efforts, we wrote a letter to the editor in support of his request that Southwest High School change its mascot and name. That brought us together into a working relationship.

Other groups and individuals, both locally and on a national level, have added to the chorus calling for change. Their stories are part of the fabric of this history, too. But this account focuses primarily on the three groups mentioned above. Their work, while sometimes controversial and ridiculed as trivial, laid the groundwork for a sweeping change in perception by school administrators, school board members, alumni, students, sports enthusiasts, and the media. The misuse of Indian images, so deeply ingrained within the majority culture, began to change. Many public schools re-named their teams and adopted new mascots. Newspapers that had once criticized the movement, changed their editorial positions. Individuals who had once brushed off the issue as trivial, began to understand the pain it could cause to see one's religion, culture, and images misused as sports entertainment.

Important as these changes are, they are only very small steps down a long, long road. Education and community awareness must continue. Professional teams that use Indian names or mascots must be challenged to examine the negative affects of their actions. It is our hope that recalling the struggle will serve as a continuing impetus for change.

Pat Helmberger

TABLE OF CONTENTS

Chapter 1

BREAKING THE SILENCE

Since the accidental arrival of Christopher Columbus to these shores, non-Indians have shaped and re-shaped images of American Indians. The "noble savage", the "wild warrior", the "pagan", the "drunken derelict", the "dependent reservation dweller" are among those images. Novelists, movie producers, merchants, and even environmentalists have used stereotypes of American Indians to sell their products or ideas. The cigar store Indian and Tonto the Lone Ranger's grunting sidekick, are among them. But perhaps no group has done more to degrade and insult Indian people than have sports organizations with team names such as Braves, Redskins, Indians, Chiefs, Blackhawks, Mohawks, and others. Those names are invariably accompanied by feathered headdresses, face and body paint, fake war whoops and dances, tomahawks, leather fringes, assorted guttural sounds, and drums beating imagined Indian music. Many American Indians and non-Indians have cringed at the obvious misuse of Indian cultures and religious symbols and icons in the name of sports at all levels: high school, college, and professional. Some American Indian parents suspected that their children tended to hide their hurt and embarrassment when they saw their culture and religion degraded on the playing field or gym floor.

In Minnesota in 1986, 50 public high schools used a form of American Indian identification for their teams and mascots.[1] According to data from the Department of Education, only a handful of those high schools had a population of ten American Indian students or more.[2]

In August, 1986, the mascot issue surfaced in a very public way. Three students at St. Cloud State University in Minnesota, Steven Brenhaug, Tracy Roel, and Karen Skaja, took offense at the fake Indian cheerleaders and howling mascot at the nearby Sauk Rapids Rice Public High School.[3] They believed that such behavior mocked American Indians and they wrote letters of protest to the school which had used an Indian mascot since 1915 but had had few, if any, American Indian team members or students.[4] Brenhaug, of Norwegian and Swedish heritage, and one of the complaining students, said, "I had grown up in Sartell, Minnesota, a small town close to Sauk Rapids. A lot of my friends went to the Sauk Rapids school so I saw first hand all the fake "Indian" behavior that was going on. I was offended by it then, but after I began taking

1

September 5, 1986

Superintendent
Sauk Rapids Schools
520 Sauk Rapids
Sauk Rapids, Minnesota 56379

Dear Colleague:

We recently heard on WCCO Radio about the Sauk Rapids High School pep squad cheers and cheerleaders outfits, and we are concerned. We applaud your asking for community response to the situation of the cheerleaders who are dressed in "Indian" dress and urging the audience to give "War Whoops" as yells. As multi-cultural resource teachers, we feel this practice is disrespectful to Native Americans and their culture.

We object to the choice of "Indian" dress and cheers because:

1. This practice does not give dignity to human beings who are proud of their culture and contributions to America. Rather it portrays American Indians as less than human.

2. It portrays American Indians as violent and warlike which perpetuates media and other stereotypes of the first Americans who have made and are making significant contributions to Minnesota and America.

3. It is an inaccurate portrayal of American Indian dress and customs.

As educators who value all students and respect the cultural diversity and heritage of all students, we encourage termination of the "Indian" theme from your high school sports events.

Linda Garrett
Linda Garrett, Coordinator of Multicultural Education

Nance Corkrum Derby
Nance Corkrum Derby, Multicultural Resource Teacher

Maxine Gaines
Maxine Gaines, Multicultural Resource Teacher

Maria C. Rocha
Maria Rocha, Multicultural Resource Teacher

Jean H. Takeshita
Jean Takeshita, Multicultural Resource Teacher

2

State of Minnesota

INDIAN AFFAIRS COUNCIL

August 29, 1986

Mr. Jerry Hartley
Superintendent of Schools
Sauk Rapids-Rice School District #47
Box 520
Sauk Rapids, MN 56373

Dear Mr. Hartley:

I would ask that your school district discontinue the use of Indians as school mascots.

We reject the position that this practice somehow shows respect for us or our culture. The adage that imitation is the highest form of flattery is valid only in direct correlation to the accuracy of portrayal.

I understand that we have been your mascot since 1915. At that period of time we were considered the "Vanishing Americans" with our extinction imminent. I must assume we were adopted as a historical relic; respect for that which was to be no more. Times change and so must attitudes.

To continue to stereotype Indians as one-dimensional, historic figures only brings discredit upon your district, denies us our validity as a viable society within twentieth-century America, and effectively steals from us our humanity.

If relegation of an entire race of people to the status of mascot is respectful and accuracy of portrayal the key ingredient; does it not logically follow that out of respect for us your district should advocate a fifty (50) percent dropout rate? We, as Indian people, see very little respect there either, but tragically it reflects accuracy of portrayal.

It is a sad commentary that Indian people alone must share the dubious honor of mascots along with lower animal forms and inanimate objects. Aretha Franklin's hit record R-E-S-P-E-C-T could become a school pep song, but not not if done in black face, tap dancing a watermelon down the football field. Without accuracy of portrayal, there is no respect.

As Indian people we are only too aware of the meager treatment we receive in school curriculum. While insensitive stereotyping causes our children pain, it works a greater disservice upon non-Indian children. Indian children learn that stereotyping is a social dysfunction; non-Indian children never do.

Indian history, Vietnam, and currently South Africa should make all of us aware that a society can justify any action against another if they are first viewed as a little less than human.

We would respectfully request that your school district discontinue using Indian people as school mascots, and that you join our effort and actively support statewide voluntary compliance. Thank you in advance for your consideration.

Sincerely,

Donald G. Gurnoe Jr.

Donald G. Gurnoe Jr.
Indian Affairs Council

DGG/lk

cc: State Board of Education

American history courses and realizing what really happened to Indian people, I became more offended."[5] When the protest became public, the school board reacted by requesting input on the mascot question, especially from Indian people.[6] Responses came from parents, Indian organizations, human rights committees, and other school districts, all explaining the negative effects of such a mascot. Staff members of The Multicultural Resource Center of the St. Paul Public Schools addressed a letter to the superintendent of the Sauk Rapids Schools explaining the negative aspects of the mascot: "1. It treats American Indians as objects rather than human beings. 2. It portrays American Indians as warlike and violent. 3. It is an inaccurate portrayal of American Indian dress and customs. 4. It perpetuates stereotypes."[7]

The Indian Affairs Council of the State of Minnesota, headquartered in Bemidji, also sent a strongly worded letter, dated August 29, 1986, and signed by member Donald G. Gurnoe, Jr., saying, "We reject the position that this practice somehow shows respect for us or our culture....It is a sad commentary that Indian people alone must share the dubious honor of mascots along with lower animal forms and inanimate objects...society can justify any action against another if they are first viewed as a little less than human." Brenhaug was invited by a Sauk Rapids social studies teacher to discuss the mascot issue with the students. "The reactions were mixed. Some students understood but others indicated that the mascot had been okay for their parents and they didn't understand why suddenly it was wrong for them," he recalled.[8]

The Minnesota Civil Liberties Union (MCLU) learned about the Sauk Rapids complaint through an August 28, 1986, newspaper article in the *St. Cloud Daily Times*. MCLU executive director, Dr. Matthew Stark, saw the use of Indian mascots as an issue of the Fourteenth Amendment of the U.S. Constitution, which guarantees every person equal protection of the law.[9] He believed that such protection was missing from the public schools when American Indian students were humiliated by the government's use of Indians as mascots, especially when non-Indian students and school staff simplistically equated Indian cultural attributes with athletic prowess and spirit. Stark, who had become MCLU's executive director in September, 1973, had served on the Governor's Human Rights Commission since the mid 1950s and had been a member of its Indian Affairs Committee. As a University of Minnesota assistant professor and coordinator of human relations programs, he had served as the advisor to American Indian students at the U of M and developed and directed an educational project on the White Earth Indian Reservation involving U of M students during the summers of 1964 to 1969. He understood the mascot issue and was anxious to test it.[10]

In order to do that, the MCLU staff needed the approval of its board of directors that this issue met constitutional standards of relevance for the MCLU. Then the staff could litigate with a volunteer attorney on behalf of a client of Indian heritage or lobby the issue on behalf of Indian parents as a way of giving them a redress of grievances. One of the MCLU goals would be to educate Minnesotans about the demeaning impact of using American Indian symbols, icons, and names as mascots of public high school athletic teams.

Stark had initiated a foundations-funded MCLU program of hiring minority law students to assist MCLU legal counsels.[11] Susan Aasen, a member of the Lac Courte Oreilles Band of Lake Superior Chippewa Indians, was one of them. She had distinguished herself at the William Mitchell College of Law in St. Paul by receiving an Outstanding Student Merit Award, a Certificate of Commendation from Governor Rudy Perpich for volunteerism, and an American Indian Cultural Program Recognition Award from the University of Minnesota.[12] Before long she became deeply involved in the MCLU Indian mascot project, helping to formulate a strong case to present to the MCLU board. In January, 1987, Stark took the complaint to the MCLU Board of Directors and received permission to move ahead on the issue.[13]

The staff began by requesting from the State Department of Education a list of public schools with American Indian mascots and nicknames. There were 50 of them with names including Indians, Warriors, Braves, Chiefs, Blackhawks, Mohawks, and Redmen. Non-Indian mascots and cheerleaders often wore feathered headdresses, face paint and fringes, howling and grunting while performing mock Indian dances and brandishing tomahawks, knives, and bow and arrows. There seemed to be little understanding that these accouterments held great religious and cultural significance for American Indian people.

The eagle feather, for instance, has long been an important part of many American Indian cultures. It is the symbol of strength and is earned through doing a brave or great deed. So sacred is the eagle feather that a 1947 federal law prohibited anyone other than an American Indian from possessing one. For some tribes, face and body paint is spiritually meaningful. Dakota people spread yellow

Maybe Now You Know
How Native Americans Feel.

For too long, America has treated its original citizens like mascots instead of people. If you'd like to help change that, write to us at 100 N. 6th Street, Suite 554-B, Minneapolis, MN 55403 or call (612) 333-8565.

Concerned American Indian Parents

paint across their faces before they went to defend their land against intruders because it symbolized the sun's strength. Other tribes incorporate face painting in burial rites. Many religious and cultural ceremonies combine songs, drums, and dances to express the voices of the people.

Another Minnesota public school was catapulted into the mascot issue in March of 1987 when the Phil St. John family sat in the old Minneapolis public auditorium during the Region 5 high school basketball tournament. Minneapolis Southwest and Osseo public high schools were soon to meet on the gym floor. One of the young St. John boys, 8-year-old Philip, Jr., ran up and down the steps, laughing and visiting with friends. As the teams ran out on the floor, he settled in beside his dad, his eyes shining. He loved the game, as did his entire family. But his bright-eyed excitement soon changed. One of the teams, the Southwest Public High School "Indians", had just sunk a basket. Suddenly its non-Indian mascot, adorned with face paint, feathers, and fringes, began dancing and screaming in the bleachers. The young boy's face burned with anger and embarrassment.

As a proud member of the Sisseton-Wahpeton Dakota Nation, he knew the painted, screaming mascot did not share the respect he felt for his culture. His family participated in pow wows and traditional ceremonies, one of his brothers as a fancy feather dancer and another in a drum group, and he recognized the mascot's behavior as mockery of his traditions. Confused, he looked at his father and whispered, "Why is he doing that?"[14]

His father, Philip Sr., determined that night he would do something to change this long held tradition that was hurtful and demeaning to his people. A social worker and chemical dependency counselor, he understood the damage done to the egos of American Indian children as they watched non-Indian students degrade their ancient heritage. As public school students, Indian youngsters saw these antics on a weekly basis - cheerleaders dressed as so-called Indian princesses, students wearing feathers and face paint while beating drums and dancing. It left many Indian students feeling confused and belittled while non-Indian children absorbed negative images of their Indian classmates and neighbors. St. John's first step was to contact the Southwest High principal, Harlan Anderson, to let him know how his son had been affected by the incident. It wasn't long before news of the problem reached the students and controversy erupted. The school's name and logo had been chosen 47 years before, supposedly to honor American Indian people.

Students were divided on the issue and even some Indian students were opposed to removing the warrior mascot in feathered headdress and fringes. The warrior image had even been implanted in the school's floor, done in colorful mosaic. Each day, each year, thousands of feet trampled and scuffed it and St. John did not see that as an honor, either.

In an attempt to help students understand the feelings of many American Indians, St. John and other Indian parents met with them, explaining how it felt to see their cultures used as a sports rallying point. "Many symbols used in the sports arena are sacred to Indian cultures, such as feathered bonnets, pipes, eagle feathers and paint. Misusing them degrades and humiliates us. No school would do this to another racial group yet there seems to be no hesitation to use Indians in this way," St. John told them. He went on to explain that it is not only the mascots but the perceptions behind the mascots that really hurt. Those perceptions often present American Indians as violent, primitive, and ignorant, frozen in time.

St. John's next visit was to the Minneapolis School Board's public meeting, where Mary Jane Smetanka, a *Star Tribune* newspaper reporter, listened to him present his views on the issue. She quoted St. John as saying, "I think the time has now come to make some obvious changes...." What impression do you think the general public would have if St. Louis Park High School was called the Jews, North High School was called the Negroes, or Edison High School was called the Polacks?"[15]

The staff at the National Conference of Christians and Jews, (NCCJ), Minnesota-Dakotas Region, read the article and knew this was a cause they wanted to support. In a letter to the editor published on May 15, Director Paul Sand and associate director, Pat Helmberger,[16] encouraged the school to make the change. As a result of that letter, St. John called the NCCJ staff to thank them for their support. After several meetings and discussions of the issue, they formed a working relationship. At the time, both Sand and Helmberger served as members of the MCLU board of directors and were involved in the Sauk Rapids Indian mascot complaint being addressed there. That made their association with St. John a natural match.

At the same time, two young advertising agents, Lyle Wedermeyer and Pam Conboy of the Martin Williams ad agency in Minneapolis had also read the article. They contacted Phil St. John and offered to do a public service poster using St. John's imaginary school team names. When the poster was completed, Phil St. John and his colleague, Fred Veilleux, an Ojibway and Concerned American Indian Parent (CAIP)[17] member, and Pat Helmberger walked over to the ad agency, just a few blocks from the NCCJ office, to see it for the first time. Against a gray cement background four sports pennants stood out in tempered contrast. Three are imaginary: the Pittsburgh Negroes, the Kansas City Jews, and the San Diego Caucasians. Separated slightly from the first three is the authentic Cleveland Indians baseball team pennant, with the grinning cartoon face of an American Indian. Beneath it are the simple words, "Maybe now you know how Native Americans feel." Within days the story of St. John, accompanied by the dramatic poster, caught the attention of the media across the nation and especially in Minnesota.

Southwest High, after staff and student meetings, agreed that the name "Indians" was no longer appropriate for their school. They believed that along with the elimination of the name the cultural abuses associated with it would also disappear. In June of 1987 the Southwest High Indians were officially retired and the team was re-named The Lakers.[18] Stark and the MCLU board greeted the news with jubilation. They had followed the controversy with great interest, coming as it did, on the heels of the Sauk Rapids school mascot complaint. Before long, the lobbying and legal expertise of the MCLU, guided by Stark, and the personal mission of St. John would join forces to reshape Minnesota history.

Chapter 2

AN ALLIANCE OF CHANGE

MCLU legal intern, Susan Aasen, began investigating the background facts needed to make a solid legal case. During the early months of 1987 she contacted public school officials asking for a list of all schools using Indian names/mascots. Then she pulled together a list of American Indian attorneys who might represent the mascot litigation. By November she had gathered much of the data needed and had written a document that laid out the constitutional issues that helped establish a firm legal foundation.[19]

One question she raised in her survey was, "Does the use of Indian mascots' symbols by State High School teams violate the rights of American Indians under United States Civil Rights laws?" She prefaced her legal interpretation with a review of an article written by Professor Charles R. Lawrence III, an African American.[20] He recalled the book *Little Black Sambo* and the feelings of shame and panic he felt as a child when he and his classmates read the book and saw the stereotypical caricatures presented. He experienced similar feelings about the 1950s national radio program "Amos and Andy" and concluded that he is a victim of our culture's deeply rooted racism. "People of color," he points out, "are subjected to unconscious racism, exerted by non-minorities, due to their cultural upbringing and symbols such as Sambo and the Amoses." The use of the Sambo restaurant signs had been challenged in Rhode Island by that state's Urban League, under the Public Accommodations portion of the Civil Rights Law. The Rhode Island Commission for Human Rights, in 1981, concluded that the signs hurt African Americans, and ordered them removed.

Similarly, according to Susan Aasen's report, American Indians suffer through the use of negative images by sports teams. It dehumanizes them and continues the stereotype of wild savages howling and brandishing tomahawks. While this issue had never been challenged in a court of law, MCLU executive director Stark, and MCLU volunteer attorney, Lucinda Jesson, from the law firm of Oppenheimer Wolff & Donnelly, believed that the case was strong. Now all they needed was a client. Experience told MCLU staff that clients often become targets of harassment and ridicule because they were usually challenging a community-accepted practice such as state sponsored prayer or religious songs at Christmas in public schools. In this instance, the organization's legal action would need an Indian student who would take on the emotional issue of team mascots tied to fan devotion. One only need attend a ball game, especially during tournament time, to understand the intensity of feelings associated with mascots and public high school team names. They were determined to search for someone who was willing to take this daring stand.

Stark and Aasen began by contacting Indian people such as Clyde Bellecourt[21], Elaine Martin Salinas[22], Will Antell[23], Phil St. John, and Ruth Meyers[24], asking them to be on the lookout for an American Indian student who attended one of the offending public schools. "We looked for two years but had no luck. Most of the schools with Indian mascots or names had few or no Indian students. Those Indian students either were not interested in the issue or they or their parents feared retaliation if they should become a client. Emotions ran high," Stark recalled.[25]

While the client search expanded, CAIP and the MCLU decided to join forces in asking the Minnesota State Board of Education to take the unprecedented step of demanding that Minnesota public schools change their Indian mascots and names. St. John contacted Ruth Meyer, an Ojibway woman from Duluth, Minnesota, and a State Board of Education member. She suggested he speak with Ted Suss, who served as administrator of the board. Suss advised caution in their approach. "Let's take a strong moral position without force of law," he said. A resolution would do that in contrast to a mandate which would force compliance.[26]

On May 9, 1988, a resolution co-written by Aasen, Stark, and St. John, was presented to, discussed, and accepted by the Board. It read in part, "Now, Therefore be it resolved that the Minnesota State Board of Education finds the use of mascots, emblems, or symbols depicting the American Indian or any other cultural or racial group unacceptable. Be it further resolved: That no school district in the State of Minnesota shall have a mascot, namesake, official symbol, team name, newspaper, yearbook, or other official group or publication bearing the name of any ethnic, racial, tribal, or religious group...."[27] This historic resolution was then passed on to the Minnesota Department of Education which, in turn, sent it to school districts throughout the state.

In many communities and schools where Indian mascots were used, the news stoked anger and resentment toward what some people believed were "outside forces" imposing a political agenda. Even though Suss believed the resolution was not a mandate, schools felt pressure to conform. And as the debates began in communities around the state, local media picked up the story. Minnesota was setting a precedent and the issues surrounding it were both emotional and complex. Many non-Indians were convinced that the use of Indian names for mascots and teams was an honor they bestowed upon American Indian people. Indian people, on the other hand, usually saw it as an insult and believed that no other ethnic group would be so maligned without a public outcry and legal remedy. Some American Indian people, however, including Darrell "Chip" Wadena, tribal chairman of the White Earth Indian Reservation, supported the use of Indian mascots and names. Dr. Will Antell, an Ojibway from White Earth Indian Reservation and, in 1988, the State Director of Equal Educational Opportunities in the State Department of Education, questioned the "honor" excuse. "We have a team named The Gophers. We don't honor gophers. We shoot them. Indians have always been portrayed as less than human, always a warrior, never a kind and loving person," he said.[28]

Former MCLU executive director, Jodi Marie Cramsie[29], now an attorney in the state of Washington, holds a similar view. "There may be no malice to begin with, but to continue using Indians as mascots after Indian people have indicated that it is harmful, that is the real problem. Schools that do that have more to answer for. They can't claim naivete and innocence any longer and they need to be challenged to explain just how they are honoring Indian people by using them as mascots," she said. Some Indian people said that if honoring them was the goal, that could best be done by stopping the use of Indian mascots. But traditions die hard when they have been in place for generations and stereotypical Indian images were so ingrained in society that many people were unable to understand how deeply hurtful they were.

Minnesota State Board of Education

705 Capitol Square Building, 550 Cedar Street, St. Paul, MN 55101 (612) 297-1925

May 19, 1998

Matthew Stark
Associate Executive Director
Minnesota Civil Liberties Union
1021 West Broadway
Minneapolis, MN

Dear Mr. Stark:

On behalf of the Minnesota State Board, I wish to express our most sincere thank you to the Minnesota Civil Liberties Union as an organization and you personally, for the efforts which led to the State Board of Education adoption of the Indian mascot resolution. A copy of the resolution is enclosed with this letter.

I know from discussions with you, other staff of the Minnesota Civil Liberties Union, and the Concerned American Indian Parents leadership, that the Minnesota Civil Liberties Union has been involved in this issue for a very long time and provided assistance to the Concerned American Indian Parents in planning a strategy which resulted in the passage of this resolution. The board is also aware of the tremendous amount of practical and political advice which made their success with the State Board possible.

It should also be noted that Susan Aasen, an intern with the Civil Liberties Union, provided considerable help to the Concerned American Indian Parents, both in the drafting of the actual resolution language, in presenting that language to the State Board of Education, and in assuring that all necessary tasks were completed so the item could be considered by the State Board.

The Minnesota Civil Liberties Union is to be commended for its continued willingness to undertake difficult and often unpopular tasks. The willingness to stay with a project until it is resolved, and to assist individuals and organizations who otherwise would not be able to approach and effectively impact change in government agencies is also a valuable service even though it may in some instances seem a nuisance to government officials.

Once again, please accept a most sincere thank you from the entire Minnesota State Board of Education.

Sincerely,

Ted L. Suss, Administrator
State Board of Education

TLS:mhSB27-46
Enclosure

14

URGING THE ELIMINATION OF THE USE OF RACIALLY DEROGATORY MASCOTS, SYMBOLS, OR EMBLEMS IN SCHOOLS THROUGHOUT THE STATE OF MINNESOTA.

WHEREAS, the use of Indian (and similar designations) mascots, emblems, or symbols depicting the American Indian in Minnesota schools is offensive to people of American Indian culture and American Indian religious traditions, and such depiction perpetuates negative racial stereotypes of the American Indian, and

WHEREAS, the practice of using mascots, emblems, or symbols disparages the ethnic heritage of American Indian students in the public education system where students are entitled to a quality educational environment regardless of race or color.

NOW THEREFORE BE IT RESOLVED, the Minnesota State Board of Education finds the use of mascots, emblems, or symbols depicting the American Indian culture or race unacceptable, and

BE IT FURTHER RESOLVED, it is the desire of the State Board of Education that no school district in the state of Minnesota shall have a mascot, namesake, official symbol, team name, newspaper, yearbook, or any official group or publication bearing the name of any American Indian symbol or cultural reference. Academic classes and/or clubs such as American Indian history, American Indian culture, Black history, or Black culture which are specifically aimed at exploring these issues are not discouraged through this resolution, and

BE IT FURTHER RESOLVED, the Minnesota State Board of Education encourages all board of education in the various Minnesota school districts to immediately commence or proceed to remove such mascots, emblems, or symbols from the public education system.

BE IT FURTHER RESOLVED, that the State Board of Education states its intention to review the progress made by public schools in fulfilling this resolution. This review is to take place at the State Board's December 1988 meeting.

This resolution approved by the State Board of Education this 10th Day of May 1988.

Marjorie Johnson

Marjorie Johnson, President
State Board of Education

TLS:mhSB17-46
5/10/88

Chapter 3

CONFRONTING PREJUDICE WITH A POSTER

The tradition of using Indians as mascots was being challenged on another front, too, as the pennant poster carrying that painful message gained national attention in February, 1988. *Sports Illustrated* magazine had featured an article about St. John along with a picture of the poster. "Switchboard operators at the magazine headquarters were flooded with calls from readers wanting to know how to get one," Pat Helmberger, then with the NCCJ, recalled. "They referred them to us at the National Conference of Christians and Jews in Minneapolis. We were serving as the poster clearinghouse then, and orders began coming in from literally around the world." she said. When *Sports Illustrated* printed the name and address of the NCCJ in the subsequent month's magazine, it was forced to hire temporary staff to help send out the 1000 posters that were ordered.

The NCCJ and CAIP had decided to keep the cost of the posters at about $5.00 so that everyone who wanted one could have it. That meant that the posters had to be subsidized and re-ordered. But with few dollars in the bank, they needed help in raising money to pay for printing costs. "We decided to have a fundraiser at my home," Helmberger recalled. "It was a potluck dinner. I invited all my friends and political allies and asked for contributions for the cause. Members of CAIP were the honored guests as well as the artists who designed the poster. Matt Stark from the MCLU was there and of course Paul Sand, NCCJ Executive Director. It was a great evening and we raised half the cost of the next printing." The poster had, indeed, caught the imagination of people who perhaps had felt uncomfortable with the misuse of Indian cultures but had not been able to put it into words. Now there was little need of words. In its simple, direct way, the poster had voiced the pain in a picture.

Despite the requests from CAIP for mascot and team name changes, the professional teams such as the Washington Redskins (football), the Atlanta Braves (baseball), and the Cleveland Indians (baseball), refused to consider such a move. Cleveland owners reminded folks that their team was named in honor of Louis Sockalexis, a Penobscot Indian from Maine, and the first American Indian to play major league baseball.[30] The Atlanta Braves, with their eerie chants and tomahawk chop, claimed that because Indian people were employed in making the styrofoam tomahawks, they were fulfilling an economic need. Washington Redskins football team owner, Jack Kent Cooke, in a letter to St. John dated January 15, 1988, said, "I find it difficult to accept your statement that the name "Redskins" is racist, derogatory and demeaning to the American Indian." He ended the letter with these words, "Basically, I want you to know that I'm totally out of sympathy with your project."

Tim Giago of the *Lakota Times* newspaper[31] attempted to help Cooke understand the issue by suggesting that he rename the team "Blackskins." "Spectators could paint their faces black, put on Afros, don colorful dashikis and cavort around the football field like a bunch of wild savages," he wrote.[32] Such analogies became commonplace in the meetings, news articles, and editorials that were part of the discussion of this issue. It seemed that the hurt could be understood only by replacing Indian people with another ethnic group, such as African Americans, Jews, or Hispanics. Many American Indians believe the misuse of their images and cultures is so pervasive that the majority community simply does not see the damage in it. Yet they can understand how an African American might feel about being called "nigger" or "blackskin", or a Jew being called a "kike". Indian scholars see the contrast: People who would be outraged by racial slurs against other ethnic minorities barely blink when American Indians are demeaned.[33]

Despite the recalcitrance of professional athletic teams, St. John received letters of encouragement from around the nation. Some of the responses carried poignant messages of thanks: Tribal chairman, Hartford Shegonee, from the Forest County Potawatomi Community in Wisconsin wrote, "Your cause is a worthy one which has, until this point, been neglected....For our children, who see their culture used with such blatant disregard, this is especially important." The National Indian Education Association in Washington, D. C., sent a letter of support, dated April 12, 1988. The Department of Civil Rights in Minneapolis, expressed similar sentiments in a letter dated April 13, 1988. There seemed to be a growing awareness that this was indeed a vital human rights issue that needed to be addressed.

NATIONAL INDIAN EDUCATION ASSOCIATION

April 12, 1988

Concerned American Indian Parents
100 North 6th Street
Suite 532-B
Minneapolis, MN 55403

To Whom It May Concern:

The National Indian Education Association strongly opposes the use of any derogatory nick names, caricatures or symbols that depict racist references and themes of Indian tribes and people. This action was taken by the Board of Directors in the January, 1988 quarterly meeting in Tulsa, Oklahoma.

If you have any questions please feel free to call our office at (202) 835-3001 or you can contact me at (406) 395-4291.

Sincerely,

Edward Parisian
President

Chapter 4

CHANGES AND CHALLENGES

While the NCCJ was sending the message on a poster and the MCLU continued preparing for its lawsuit and expanding its lobbying, the CAIP met with the Minneapolis Park and Recreation Board to ask them to end the use of American Indian names and symbols for their city-sponsored youth programs. On April 13, 1988, the CAIP's efforts met with success when the Board adopted such a policy. It read in part, "...no program, event or activity offered by the Minneapolis Park and Recreation Board will use any ethnic, religious or racial names or symbols which may in the opinion of those groups create or perpetuate stereotypes which distort or degrade such groups."[34]

In February, 1989, the State Board of Education sent a letter to school districts asking for a progress report on their mascot name changes. By July of 1989, it was obvious that many school districts were ignoring the State Board of Education's request. Only twelve districts had agreed to change. Twenty-six districts did not even respond to the board's February, 1989 letter asking them to change. Sate board members were angry at the districts' foot-dragging and asked Dr. Antell to contact the 26 schools which did not respond. He concluded that many districts were waiting for the threatened lawsuit by the MCLU while other districts watched for further action by the Board of Education.[35] At a public meeting in Monticello to discuss the mascot issue, Antell's job was threatened by an influential public official who questioned Antell's right to "come into my district and cause problems." [36]

At Humboldt Public High School in St. Paul, at a meeting especially convened to discuss the misuse of Indian cultures and religions, Phil St. John explained that racist stereotypes often accompany Indian mascots. Despite the MCLU's threatened lawsuit, the State Education Department's request, and an order from the St. Paul School Board to abolish the Indian mascot, students and alumni were determined to save it. Hundreds gathered, some carrying signs and banners, shouting their support for the long-standing tradition. Alumni seemed more angry than the students over the feared loss. Even some American Indian students supported the logo and threatened a hunger strike if it were removed.[37] St. John recalls this as CAIP's most difficult battle.[38]

In contrast, some schools, such as Park Public High in Cottage

Grove, quietly began to phase out its Indian mascot, lessening the likelihood of confrontation. It took five years to completely eliminate the symbols that adorned school letterhead, yearbooks, and some sports paraphernalia. During this time, the school initiated an educational project about American Indian cultures to help students understand that the headdress worn by their mascot is really a sacred symbol and not one that should be used in sports events. The Prairie Island Mdewakanton Sioux Community, which operates Treasure Island Casino, was so impressed by the school that they asked if they could visit. When they did, they brought along a $10,000 check to help defray costs of the change.[39]

In Sauk Rapids, where the issue had first surfaced, student council members pushed for a team name change. In an undated letter to the school board, they wrote, "As a school district we have adopted a mission statement that says we are aiming at...producing...learners who will excel in a high-tech, global society, and developing community programs to promote multicultural issues." The letter questioned the sincerity of the mission statement if the school continued ignoring the Indian nickname issue. It was nine years from the initial complaint before the Sauk Rapids Indians became the "Storm".[40]

By early 1989 the MCLU decided it was time, with or without a client, to escalate their efforts regarding public school use of Indian mascots. On January 19, the organization sent letters to 50 Minnesota public schools that had not yet changed their athletic team's mascot stating that a lawsuit would be commenced against them if they did not make the changes suggested by the State Board. The letter, signed by Jesson, MCLU volunteer attorney, included this paragraph: "Use of an Indian mascot develops and perpetuates racist perceptions of Native Americans, particularly when mascots are used in connection with athletic events where students may dress like Indians, howl, give out war whoops and use symbols, such as feathers and headdresses, which have religious and cultural significance for Native Americans. Indians are a race of people with a separate culture and religion that must be respected. Indians should not be used as substitutes for animal symbols. The simple act of having an Indian as a mascot is, in itself, demeaning."[41]

Since the summer of 1988, the MCLU knew that some Indian leaders, particularly Chip Wadena, tribal chairman of the White Earth Indian Reservation and chair of the Minnesota Chippewa Tribal Council, along with his political allies, had voiced objection to the MCLU and the state Board of Education and immediately had

The Hibbing Daily Tribune

VOLUME 51
NUMBER 22
USPS 235-120

HIBBING, MINNESOTA 55746, WEDNESDAY EVENING, JANUARY 25, 1989

FOUR SECTIONS
PRICE
THIRTY-FIVE CENTS

ACLU on warpath over Indian nicknames

ST. PAUL, Minn. (UPI) – The Minnesota Civil Liberties Union has sent a letter to 54 schools telling them to change their Indian-theme name or face a possible lawsuit.

The state Board of Education adopted a resolution last year asking the state public schools to drop the Indian nicknames.

The MCLU said the Indian nicknames such as "Warriors" and "Braves" violate state laws and the United States Constitution. The letter said the use of an Indian mascot develops and perpetuates racist perceptions of Native Americans.

Twenty-two schools in Minnesota have the team name "Indian" and is the third most popular team name in the state. Fourteen are called the "Warriors," six the "Braves" and two the "Chiefs." Other names include the "Mohawks" and "Redmen."

MCLU volunteer attorney Lucinda E. Jesson wrote the letter.

"Use of an Indian mascot develops and perpetuates racist perceptions of Native Americans," Jessen said in the letter, "particularly when mascots are used in connection with athletic events where students may dress like Indians, howl, give our war whoops and use symbols, such as feathers and head dresses, which have religious and cultural significance for Native Americans."

She said the continued use of Indian mascots, nicknames and emblems not only flouts the Board of Education resolution, but violates the equal protection guarantees of the Constitution, federal and state civil rights laws and public accommodation laws. She said the Constitution and society would not permit the use of blacks, whites, Jews or other races as mascots.

In a related action last week, the State Board of Education recommended that Education Commissioner Ruth Randall write a letter to the superintendents asking them to drop the Indian team names.

Fred Veilleux, a member of the Concerned American Indian Parents, said he hopes Randall will inform his group within a month whether she intends to write the letter. He raised the mascot issue with the board last year.

In May, Minneapolis Southwest High School changed its team name from the Indians to the Lakers. Other schools with Indian team names have failed to take similar action.

Henry Sibley Senior High students had a debate last spring with representatives of the Concerned American Indian Parents. They put the issue to a vote of the students grades nine through 12 who voted to retain "Warriors," saying it was a way to honor Indians.

21

begun lobbying that agency to "water-down" its strong objection to the use of Indian mascots in Minnesota high schools.

The *Hibbing Daily Tribune* used the insensitive headline, "ACLU on warpath over Indian nicknames," to describe the threatened suit.[42] Opposition to the MCLU and its lawsuit threats came from Wadena who claimed in a February 8, 1989, report, that Stark and the MCLU had never asked his input on a question affecting him and his people. He supported the use of Indian names and mascots on the reservations where most, if not all, students and sports team members were Indian.[43] On February 16, 1989, in the *Detroit Lakes Tribune*, Wadena continued his attacks on efforts to eliminate Indian mascots.[44] The days and months of controversy kept the issue before the public. In a *Star Tribune* article on March 6, 1989, reporter Norman Draper, wrote...."But when the Minnesota Civil Liberties Union (MCLU) and the State Department of Education put pressure on every Minnesota public high school with an Indian-related nickname to change it, that likely marked the first such effort ever launched in the nation....Some superintendents reported strong community opposition to the proposed changes, which in some cases will sweep away traditions that have lasted generations."

St. John came to the MCLU's defense in a letter to the editor dated March 14, 1989, printed in *Anishinabe Dee-Bah-Gee-Mo-Win* in which he stated that CAIP was the group that initiated action on the mascot issue, not the MCLU. He characterized Wadena as "a person that is caught between two cultures, one of which he has lost sight of and the other of which he is not a full member."[45] Two days later on March 16, the Leech Lake Indian Reservation Business Committee adopted a resolution asking "The MCLU and the State Board of Education to reverse their respective decisions and to work with the Minnesota Chippewa Tribes and the Minnesota American Indian Education Advisory Council, and...refrain from attempting to speak for all Indian people without consultation of the elected tribal officials."

A *St. Paul Pioneer Press* cartoon, on March 23, 1989, depicted the MCLU as an overweight man carrying a sign reading "Drop School Team Indian names OR ELSE!" Behind him is a member of the Leech Lake Indian Reservation saying, "Huh..it never bothered me." Then, in an editorial dated March 27, 1989, the *Star Tribune* suggested that the MCLU drop its lawsuit. "The MCLU stand on this issue has never made good sense....If the MCLU belongs in this case, it should be on the other side, affirming the right of students and their educators to choose nicknames even if their choices offend

23

Educational Institutions Promote Racist Attitudes

by Fred Veilleux

The Concerned American indian Parents (CAIP) organization and the National Coalition on Racism in Sports and the Media (NCRSM) were formed as a means to address society's exploitation of Indian culture, Indian identity and Indian people as portrayed by athletic team mascots and fan behavior. There are approximately 1500 high schools, 90 colleges and universities and a countless number of public parks across America where mascots of American Indians are used, not to mention the five professional sport teams that do the same.

• • • •

It took us one year to convince the State Board of the inappropriateness of using the name of a race of people for a school mascot, and in 1988, the Board issued a letter to all school districts in question urging them to eliminate their use of Indian related names for mascots. We were joined in this effort by the Minnesota Civil Liberties Union (MCLU), which took the position that it is unconstitutional to single out a race group in a public school for anything other than an educational purpose. Therefore, the schools in question were discriminating against American Indian students and were in violation of the Fourteenth Amendment. The MCLU threatened to file suit against those schools who refused to change their names.

Since that time, 27 or 50 schools in question changed their name either voluntarily or by order of their local school board. One of the reasons the remaining schools stopped short of changing their mascot names was that the President of the Minnesota Chippewa Tribe, Darrel "Chip" Wadena, stated publicly to the media, his criticism of the State Board of Education's resolution to eliminate Indian names because the Board had not consulted tribal officials.

Wadena who is also tribal chairman of the White Earth reservation, stated further that the reservation tribal council passed a resolution supporting the Mahnomen school district in retaining it's nickname the "Indian." Because of Wadena's political position, the public assumed he spoke for all Indian people.

and their educators to choose nicknames even if their choices offend some people...."

Although Stark was hurt by the reaction of the press, he said, "I took comfort in the advice I had gotten years ago from Roger Baldwin, founder of the American Civil Liberties Union. He encouraged us to be vigorous and make strong and forceful statements to the media in spite of criticism by cartoonists and editorial writers," Stark said. In that spirit, he defended the MCLU in a commentary printed in the April 1, 1989, issue of the *Star Tribune* by saying that public schools violated the Equal Protection Clause of the 14th Amendment when they chose Indian names for sports teams. He concluded the article by stating that "Being at the forefront when rights are violated, before they become "popular" and when there is risk, is what the MCLU has stood for in the past and continues to stand for today."[46]

On March 14, the Steele County Women Trial Lawyers Association held a public forum on the use of the school name "Owatonna Indians" in Owatonna. One of the spokespersons was Barb Anderson from the Upper Sioux Agency. She was joined by Joe Campbell and George Estes, from the Prairie Island Indian Community. They told students, community members, and school officials that they objected to the trivialization of their most sacred symbols. "Each one of those feathers on an Indian head dress have a meaning," Estes explained. Anderson criticized the use of fringe on cheerleader costumes, "In our culture each fringe on a woman's dress represents tears. As a woman matures she earns the right to wear fringe on her dress. It shows that she has experienced some suffering in her life."[47]

Jim Lenfestey, a graduate of Dartmouth College and a Minneapolis writer, added his thoughts to the debate in an April 23 *Star Tribune* opinion piece. "Who has the right to use, or abuse, a group's name? Only that group. Yet the truth of history is that people in power have chosen their symbols without consideration of the rights or emotions of minorities...Minnesotans should thank the MCLU for putting the state through semantic therapy, just as the Indian students did at Dartmouth 15 years ago. It has forced us all to confront our reasons for caring about Indian symbols, as opposed to real Indians, once again," he wrote.[48]

In July, 1989, Indian students at the Minneapolis Heart of the Earth Indian Survival School, expressed their feelings in an editorial published in *The Circle*, an American Indian newspaper: "Most public and private high schools have a mascot for their teams. A mascot is supposed to be a good luck charm. As the *New Expanded*

Webster Dictionary of 1988 says, 'A mascot is a thing that is supposed to bring good luck to its owner.' Indians are not good luck charms. We are human like yourself....As Indians, we are being patronized like we are an owned pet....We believe that if the white majority understood our point of view, they would willingly tear down the mascots today."

Mascots are offensive to American Indians

NOTES FROM
INDIAN COUNTRY

What is it about the word "racism" the editorial page editor of the Mitchell (S.D.) *Daily Republic*

and wearing turkey feather bonnets or by painting his face and denigrating our religious ceremonies. Do you

Star Tribune

A fight the MCLU shouldn't have picked

The Minnesota Civil Liberties Union should drop its effort to eliminate Indian nicknames from public schools. In this dispute the MCLU isn't

9/27/89

Department of Education to encourage compliance. But divergent opinions within the Indian community suggest the board and department

12/3/92

St. Paul Pioneer Press Dispatch 3/8/57   F 3B

Rights groups back team name changes

The MCLU has threatened to sue the schools if they do not change their mascot names.

Star Tribune

Give Burnsville an 'A' on Indian nicknames

Burnsville High School is the latest Minnesota school to drop an Indian nickname. The school board's commendable decision recognizes that no longer is it acceptable for white-majority schools to use symbols, often demeaning, based on a minority's traits and culture.

Star Tribune
Monday
March 6/1989

Bid to rid schools of Indian logos may be a first

MCLU, state education agency encounter compliance and resistance

MONDAY, OCTOBER 9, 1989

ST PAUL
PIONEER PRESS
DISPATCH

SCHOOL LOGOS

Don't name mascots after real-life people

Star Tribune/Tuesday/February 13/1990

Indian logos, mascots still must go

State education board hasn't 'waffled' on issue, it says

By Mary Jane Smetanka
Staff Writer

Members of the State Board of Education Monday reaffirmed their request that Minnesota schools drop such nicknames, although they don't want them used in racist ways.

State board members yesterday reaffirmed their 1988 position, saying they encourage "school districts to remove among Indians. 1988 position in the district tapped a serious a failed attempt to restore the nickname

State board member Alan Zdon said in "was inadvertently yet without board awareness, moved into the discussion materials" after board members had made it clear that they favored passive techniques to control behavior

Star Tribune
Commentary/Counterpoint 4/1/89

Indian mascots in schools violate Indian civil rights

The Minnesota Civil Liberties Union (MCLU) is continuing its support of Indian efforts to remove Indian using Indian names be stopped. Those efforts, as well as the efforts of the MCLU, are supported by the types and biased attitudes often cannot be accomplished by mere reasoned dialogue. In fact, litigation and

Chapter 5

INDIAN" MASCOTS: RESPECTFUL OR RACIST?

A mascot is described in various dictionaries as a thing, an animal, or a person thought to bring good luck. The ten most popular mascot names among American colleges are Eagles, Tigers, Cougars, Bulldogs, Warriors, Lions, Panthers, Indians, Wildcats, and Bears. As is easily seen, all of the mascots are animals or birds, with the exception of Warriors and Indians. Frank Rays notes in his book, *What's in a Nickname?* that if all the names associated with American Indians were grouped together such as Redmen, Warriors, Savages, Braves and Chiefs, they would far outnumber all other groups of nicknames.[49]

There are a variety of reasons given for using Indian names and images as team/school mascots. Honor and tradition are two of them. Other less innocent reasons cannot be ignored. America has romanticized its tragic history against Indian people, creating heroes of those who led battles against innocent inhabitants simply because they were in the way of western expansion. In their native land, they were restricted to reservations, numbed with alcohol, and made the brunt of insults, jokes, and cartoons depicting them as shiftless, drunken, and stupid. These distorted images, passed from one generation to another, helped non-Indians avoid the truth of what had happened to millions of American Indians. Under the guise of Manifest Destiny and religious conversion of the "heathen", the historic policy of the United States government was to "settle" Indian lands, to Christianize the natives, and to eliminate the use of Indian languages and the teaching of Indian cultures to the next generation of Indian children.

For all the assertions that Indian names and mascots are chosen to honor Indian people, invariably the names, logos, and antics associated with the team are insulting and belittling. Arkansas State University has teams called "Indians," and "Tomahawks," with a logo of a grotesquely grinning little Indian, flaunting a tomahawk and scalp.[50] At Pembroke State University in North Carolina, the sports teams are called "Braves" and "Lady Braves" accompanied by a drawing of an Indian in feathers and braids, waving a tomahawk, while doing a dance and war-whoop. His nose is large and he is wearing only a loincloth.[51] Montclair State College in New Jersey named their male and female players "Indians" and "Squaws".[52] Wild antics and war whoops usually accompany these nicknames.[53]

Lakota George, an Indian who grew up in South Dakota, remembers his frightening experience as a basketball player on a team called the "Indians". He recalls walking onto the gym floor of a host high school and seeing in large red letters, "Scalp the Indians." "I was scared," he admitted. "I was the only Indian on the team!" Lakota George recounted a similar incident experienced by another Indian youth. This student had attended his school's pep rally in preparation for a football game against a rival school whose mascot was an American Indian. The rally included the hanging of an Indian in effigy along with posters and banners that read "Scalp the Indians"; "Kill the Indians" and "Burn the Indians at the stake." The student, hurt and embarrassed, tore the banners down. His fellow students could not understand his pain. That was in 1962.[54] Since then, some changes have come about.

In 1970, the University of Oklahoma dropped its "Little Red" mascot. In 1971, Marquette University abolished its mascot, "Willie Wampum" and Stanford University dropped its "Indian" nickname in 1972. Dartmouth College changed in 1974 when the "Indians" team became "Big Green" after Indian students complained. In 1975 Syracuse University followed suit and ended its "Saltine Warrior" mascot.

In contrast, in 1995, the Illinois House of Representatives voted to retain the "Chief Illiniwek" mascot at the University of Illinois in Champaign. The bill was vetoed by Illinois Governor Jim Edgar. Although Edgar supports the Chief Illiniwek symbol, he believes "that its continued presence at the University should be determined on the campus - and not in the capitol."[55] Images of the "chief" abound on businesses and sports facilities and are printed on rolls of toilet paper sold in and around the University campus.

The Illinois Department of Education had been conducting an investigation into whether the mascot created a hostile environment for American Indians. In response, State Rep. Thomas Ewing threatened the Illinois Education Department's budget if it did not stop the investigation. He and ten other Illinois lawmakers wrote to Federal Education Secretary Richard Riley, urging him to affirm the University's right to have Chief Illiniwek as its symbol.[56] A *New York Times* article dated December 3, 1995, stated that the Federal Education Department ruled that the Chief Illiniwek mascot "does not create a hostile environment for Indians." Indian students vowed to continue working for the elimination of what they consider a racist symbol, according to the *New York Times*.

Another incident confirms that change comes slowly. The

Naperville Central High School's 1987 yearbook contained a page that caught the attention of the Illinois State Board of Education resulting in a recommendation that the school drop its "Redskins" name and mascot. The objectionable page included student suggestions for "87 Uses For A Dead Redskin." The uses included "redskin rug, target practice, doorstop, firewood, maggot farm, punching bag, toilet paper holder, dog feed and moosebait."[57]

Professor Clara Sue Kidwell of Choctaw and Ojibway heritage, is the director of the Native American Studies Program at the University of Oklahoma. She sees the danger in using American Indian symbols for sports mascots. While many of them are chosen to glorify the strength of Indian people, they deteriorate into something derogatory. She uses the Dartmouth College "Indian" former mascot as an example, referring to it as "the stereotypical drunken Indian". When symbols are given racial connotations in a competitive institution such as a college, they usually become offensive and it is invariably American Indians who are used in this way, she indicated.[58] She also believes that "the association of Indians with warfare in American history subtly, or not so subtly, makes a psychological connection between public school sports competitiveness and the violence and destructiveness of war."[59]

While the mascot debate went on across the country during the late 80s and early 90s, professional teams dug in their heels against any name changes. Jack Kent Cooke, owner of the Washington Redskins, and Atlanta Braves owner, Ted Turner, seemed oblivious to the hurtful behavior the team names promoted. That behavior includes this fight song "Hail to the Redskins":

> Scalp 'em, swamp 'em, we will
> Take 'um big score.
> Read 'um, weep 'um, touchdown,
> We want heap more!

Then there is the pig that Redskin fans paint red, crown with a war bonnet, and chase around the field; and there is the Tomahawk Chop done by Atlanta Brave fans, which includes Jane Fonda, owner Turner, and former President Jimmy Carter. Of the three, only Carter has lived up to the promise of refraining from this racist action in the future. Turner continues to refuse to change the name of the Atlanta Braves.

Professor Ward Churchill of the University of Colorado, wrote in his book, *Indians are us?*, that Indians in America shared the same fate as the Jews in Germany. By dehumanizing both groups, it was possible to practice genocide on them without a worldwide outcry.

It was also possible to use them in stereotypical and derogatory ways as jokes, mascots and cartoons. "One can only conclude that...Indians are (falsely) perceived as being too few, and therefore too weak, to defend themselves effectively against racist and otherwise offensive behavior." he wrote.[60]

Jill Carlson, a freshman at St. Cloud State University in 1998, wrote a paper in which she reached similar conclusions. "Another reason the Indian mascot is a racist act is the history of the Native Americans. They have suffered genocide where millions of their people were killed.... Over the centuries, the Native American population dropped to fewer than 250,000 people because of governmental policies...."[61], Carlson wrote.

Jodi Cramsie decried the fact that in the seat of our national government, we have a racist pro-sports team - the Redskins. She believes that big money rules pro-sports and the owners are not influenced by a small group of protesters.[62] Suzan Shown Harjo, of Cheyenne and Muscogee heritage, and executive director of the Morning Star Institute in Washington D.C., said, "The problem is deadly serious. These names serve to diminish an entire people....The educated white man of the 16th century engaged in a philosophical argument about whether Indians were really human beings with souls," she said. "It appears some still think we are not exactly people."[63]

European Americans have glorified those who killed Indian people through warfare, disease-infected blankets, starvation, and cultural upheaval. Popular American movies and novels have often depicted American Indians as savage, grunting warriors or as comical and childlike figures, confused by the superior technology of non-Indians. Sometimes they are shown as tragic or mystical figures facing a future in which they do not fit. It was not difficult to continue the dehumanization process so well begun, by making them into a token of good luck on the same level as tigers, lions, and bears.

"If a race of people are treated as nothing more than mascots for the fun and games of sporting teams, they will be treated with disrespect in all other walks of life."

Tim Giago. Indian Country Today

PEMBROKE STATE U. "Braves", "Lady Braves", Pembroke, N.C.

Arkansas State University State University

Indians.

TUNXIS CC "Tomahawks" Farmington, Conn.

Chapter 6

OPPOSING VIEWS FROM AMERICAN INDIANS

Some Indian people believe that reservations schools, or schools with a majority of American Indian students, should be allowed to keep their Indian mascots and names. None was more vocal or sincere than the Red Lake school district students on the Red Lake Indian Reservation in Northern Minnesota. They sent a petition to the MCLU which the school children had passed in February, 1989. expressing their feelings about their cherished Warriors name. It read in part: "Being an American Indian Warrior has been and still is a position commanding social pride and respect from our cultural heritage. Therefore, we take exception to the Minnesota Civil Liberty (sic) Union's petition concerning Red Lake for the following reasons: 1. The Red Lake Indian Reservation is a sovereign nation with its own entity. 2. The Red Lake Independent School District #38 student enrollment is 100% Red Lake Indians. 3. The team name of "WARRIORS" is original for our people and is held with great pride and respect. 4. The word Warrior is aboriginal as well as our people.[64]

Letters from individual students re-enforced the petition's argument. One student wrote that the Red Lake High School should be able to keep the name WARRIORS because the students are American Indians. "When I see the word WARRIORS for other people's mascot it doesn't seem right because the race that they are doesn't fit there (sic) school mascot or team that they are supposed to represent," she explained. Another expressed a similar attitude. "I feel it is wrong for white schools to have mascots named after Indians, but this is a school for Indians and we are proud of the name," she wrote.

Such letters touched officials at the Minnesota State Board of Education and the Minnesota Department of Education. They could well understand the sentiments of the students but their concern centered on what other, off reservation non-Indian schools, did with the mascot and name during the heated rivalry that accompanies sport events. There was very little control over the stereotypes depicted or the images portrayed. When students at competing high schools hanged Indians in effigy or used threats of scalping and burning in almost automatic reflexes to an Indian name, the concerns of some Education Department personnel and MCLU leaders appeared justified. It seemed as if Indian schools were setting themselves up for ridicule. In order to blunt some of the criticism from Indian tribal leaders, CAIP reaffirmed its support of the MCLU in a letter dated March 3, 1989. It read in part: "The MCLU has stood with us from our initial confrontation with the Minneapolis Public School System and Southwest High School. We felt that the only resolution to this concern would have to be through legal channels and the MCLU has been gracious enough to provide us with this legal assistance....Our organizational goal is to have a national elimination of negative stereotyping of American Indians and with the assistance of the MCLU, we feel that we can attain this long range goal." It was signed by St. John, CAIP's most recognizable member. [65]

In a letter dated March 31, 1989, Richard Tanner, Director of the Education Division of the Minnesota Chippewa Tribe, invited MCLU members to meet with Wadena and other tribal representatives at the Holiday Inn near the State Capitol in St. Paul to discuss the mascot issue. Stark called upon Clyde Bellecourt, an Ojibway and one of the founders of the American Indian Movement, to accompany him. "Here we would have one Indian leader talking to another Indian leader," Stark said.[66]

But even that meeting, at which Indians spoke on both sides of the issue, did not persuade the Chippewa tribal government officials to join the anti-mascot movement. They still harbored resentment toward the MCLU for asking for mascot changes without first consulting them. Despite Stark's public apology for not consulting with tribal chairman Wadena before recommending action to the MCLU board of directors and his plea for Wadena to join the effort against Indian mascots for the sake of Indian youngsters, Wadena remained adamant. Even Bellecourt's impassioned statement that "racism is everyone's business" did not sway their attitudes.

Other groups, however, did offer support to the MCLU. Among them were the American Indian Center, Minnesota; The American Indian Law Center; the National Congress of American Indians; the Association of American Indian Affairs, Inc.; the National Indian Education Association; The United Indian Nations In Oklahoma;, the Title 4 Coordinators for Indian Education in Onamia and Anoka, Minnesota; the Executive Director of the Minneapolis Department of Civil Rights; the St. Paul branch of the NAACP; the leader of the Upper Midwest Indian Center, Mpls; the St. Paul Humboldt Public High School Indian Affairs Director; Dr. Clara Sue Kidwell, then professor of American Indian Studies at the University of California at Berkeley; Ruth Meyers, Affirmative Action Co-ordinator at the

University of Minnesota's Medical School, Duluth, and an American Indian member of the State Board of Education; Dr. Will Antell, Indian Education Director in the Minnesota Department of Education; Elaine Martin Salinas, then head of the Heart of the Earth Indian Survival School in Minneapolis; and many other Indian people on various reservations in Minnesota who disagreed with the position taken by Wadena and his political allies.[67]

Spurred by Minnesota's efforts to end the stereotyping of American Indians, Michigan's Department of Civil Rights, in October, 1988, issued a report on *Use of Nicknames, Logos and Mascots Depicting Native American People in Michigan Education Institutions*. It said, "The problem of stereotyping was devastatingly clear in the media story on a joint project between Minneapolis Indian parents and the National Conference of Christians and Jews which served as the starting point for this project." It found that four colleges, 62 high schools and 33 junior high/middle schools in Michigan used Indian names and symbols. It concluded that Native Americans are the only racial group used to describe sports teams in Michigan; that logos were generally stereotypic and included several which were clearly degrading; that the prevailing images found in Indian names and logos is based on a Hollywood image of Indians: ferocious fighters, limited language skills, or primitive savages. The report suggested that even when schools change to the "noble savage" the image is still inaccurate or misused. All images are subject to common stereotyping by the public or sportswriters. Frequent use of "scalping", "burning at the stake", "little Indians" or "Injuns" in sports stories or headlines reflect an absence of sensitivity to the negative impact of this usage.[68]

The Michigan Department of Civil Rights report points to an example in the March 1988 edition of *Central Michigan Life* that carried a story entitled "Torturer". It stated that if a Central Michigan University wrestler had been a "real-life Indian, he would have taken great pleasure in collecting enemy scalps, and then drinking the blood." Those negative images, according to the report, continue "in part because media-created images of Indians have been widely accepted by the public and in part because of general public attitudes toward Indians." It also expressed concern over a potential backlash against Indian students as a result of releasing the report. Since that 97 page report was written, however, only six Michigan institutions have changed their logos and/or names related to American Indians.

Arthur Stine, legislative policy and program co-ordinator for the Michigan Department of Civil Rights, said there is still resistance to change in many communities where Indian mascots are used.

Association on American Indian Affairs, Inc.

95 Madison Avenue
New York, N.Y. 10016-7877
(212) 689-8720

Dr. Idrian N. Resnick
Executive Director
legal (2)
minnaclu.ltr
1/25/89

January 25, 1989

Mr Bob Hicks
Minnesota Civil Liberties Union
1021 West Broadway
Minneapolis, Minnesota 55411

Dear Hicks,

As per our telephone conversation and your letter of January 12, 1989, you may use the following statement in any form that is consistent with the aims of the Minnesota Civil Liberties Union's efforts to get public schools to stop using Indians and Indian symbols as mascots or names of their teams/ organizations.

The Association on American Indian Affairs, a 66 year old national, non-profit advocacy organization, supports the efforts of the Minnesota Civil Liberties Union to get public schools in the state to stop using Indian names, symbols and mascots.

We will make a small note of this work in our next issue of Indian Affairs (some recent copies of which I enclose) and we are available for future collaboration on this and other work related to Indians.

Sincerely yours,

Dr. Idrian N. Resnick
Executive Director

MINNEAPOLIS
AMERICAN INDIAN CENTER
1530 East Franklin Avenue • Minneapolis, Minnesota 55404
612-871-4555

March 10, 1989

Phil St. John
Concerned American Indian Parents
100 North 6th Street
Minneapolis, Minnesota 55403

Dear Mr. St. John:

The Minneapolis American Indian Center supports the work that your group, "Concerned American Indian Parents", has been doing to eliminate the use of American Indians as mascots at educational institutions.

Since its opening the Minneapolis American Indian Center has worked long and hard for the elimination of racism and discrimination.

We are in support of any group or organization whose purpose is to eliminate stereotypes or racism against American Indians and other minority groups.

Sincerely,

Frances Fairbanks
Executive Director

FF:cg

"We have not been very successful in making changes here and we have never taken a formal complaint," he said. When Eastern Michigan University changed its team name from "Hurons" to "Eagles," some alumni brought a lawsuit against the college, wanting to retain the "Hurons" name, but they did not prevail. The next year, the team had a great winning season and that eased some of the wounds of the mascot dispute.[69] Stine said that the use of Indians as mascots is not based on facts or history but rather on a Hollywood image of the Plains Indian: a good fighter, a savage, but never intelligent or kind. "That is what Indian kids hear about their people and that could certainly affect their self-esteem," he said.

Students at the Santa Fe, New Mexico Indian School clearly understood the damage such stereotyping could do and they wrote to the MCLU, expressing gratitude for banning Indian names for mascots. Seventh grader Kenny Weahkee, in a letter dated February 2, 1989, wrote, "It hurts us to see white fans acting like wild Indians, which we're not."

A month later, *St. Paul Pioneer Press* columnist Nick Coleman urged a change of the Warriors mascot at Henry Sibley High School in West St. Paul. In his March 14, 1989 column, "'Warriors' and Sibley don't mesh," he explained to readers that Henry Sibley, Minnesota's first governor, had become wealthy on the backs of the Dakota people. "He should be remembered for the ruthless manner in which he exploited the Dakota people of Minnesota and for his actions that helped lead to the theft of Indian land and the near genocidal destruction of Minnesota's original citizens....On Dec. 26, 1862, 38 Dakota "Warriors" were hanged in Mankato by Sibley's men. Hundreds more were sent to prison....Honoring Henry Sibley's name with a high school might simply be more evidence that we are ignorant of our past and its meaning."[70]

In March, 1989, Myron Ellis, a representative of the Leech Lake Indian Reservation's business committee, said, "We are opposed to the action of the MCLU, and we question their authority to speak on our behalf. We view the use of Indian names as a point of pride if they are used respectfully and in good taste." Wadena of the White Earth Indian Reservation agreed.[71] Eugene Boshey, chairman of the Bois Forte Indian Reservation in northeastern Minnesota, concurred with other tribal leaders. "I don't care whether it's up here in Orr, where we have the Braves, or in a Twin Cities suburb. If they take pride in the name, let them use it," he told the *Star Tribune* newspaper.[72]

Santa Fe Indian School
Middle School
P.O. Box 5335
Santa Fe, NM 87502
February 2, 1989

Carrie Orth
Executive Director
Minnesota Civil Liberties Union
1021 West Broadway
Minneapolis, Minnesota 55411

Dear Ms. Orth:

Santa Fe Indian School is an off-reservation boarding school
in Santa Fe, New Mexico. To attend the school, students must
be part Native American. There are approximately 500
students currently enrolled at SFIS, in grades 7-12. The
students are from the 19 Pueblos in New Mexico, as well as
from the Navajo and Apache tribes of New Mexico and
Arizona.

I am a Pueblo Indian and teach in the Mid School. One of my
classes is a small group of 7th graders enrolled in "Indian
Issues." While listening to "National Native News" on a
National Public Radio station, I learned of the possible suit
the Minnesota Civil Liberties Union may bring against
Minnesota public high schools using Indian names for the
athletic teams.

I developed the conflict into a unit for my 7th graders. We
spent several days discussing it. The students support your
position and wanted to write support letters for the MCLU.
Enclosed are those letters.

The learning experience was valid and especially relevant for
the students. Their awareness of a cultural issue was
heightened. Their thought processes were utilized extensively.
Their decision making skills were sharpened. The students,
not myself, came up with the idea of writing to you. Thus,
they practiced letter-writing skills as well.

I would appreciate any response you or your office could
provide to this enlightened group of students. Perhaps, you
could keep them informed as to the progress of the case.

Respectfully,

Debbie Harragarra
Teacher

41

But almost invariably the mascot depictions were degrading and the slogans used, especially by the opposing teams, were cruel. A case in point was the contest between the Owatonna high school team, the Indians, and the Albert Lea public high school football team, the Tigers, in October 1989. The Albert Lea Homecoming button was blazoned with "Ambush the Indians" along with a cartoon tiger carrying a stereotypical Indian with feathers in his hair and a rope around his body. Members of the school's Amnesty International chapter wrote a letter to Alan Root, the Albert Lea Principal, expressing their belief that the button and slogan were inappropriate. Paul Goodnature, Minnesota's 1987 Teacher of the Year, and faculty advisor to Amnesty International, personally complained to Stark about this public high school abuse of American Indians.[73]

In November, 1989, Minnesota State Representative Marcus Marsh from Sauk Rapids sent a letter to Education Commissioner Ruth Randall that stated, "I am writing to request that your Department stop harassing school districts that have Indian names." It ended with a similar request, noting "It appears that the only people who support your action is the MN Civil Liberties Union." MCLU's Stark reminded readers of the *Detroit Lakes Tribune* that "no school that has any of these names has a single course on Indian culture or Indian language." In fact, numerous public school officials in Minnesota acknowledged to Stark that for the first time they understood that the misuse of the war bonnet or other kind of headdress is sacrilegious to Indian people.[74] That understanding came about because the CAIP and MCLU had raised the mascot issue. Still, the American Indian Education Committee of the State Board of Education was swayed by the schools which wanted to keep their Indian mascots and names. Therefore, late in November of 1989, they voted to allow school districts with Indians logos to continue their use as long as it was done under certain standards of conduct. That vote was a deep disappointment to Stark and St. John.[75] Stark recalled that he walked a block from the MCLU office on West Broadway in Minneapolis to the Upper Midwest Indian Center to visit with Emily Peake, its executive director. He took comfort in her words of encouragement. "Don't worry. You are doing the right thing. All the Indians I have talked with agree that the use of Indians as team mascots is offensive," she told him.

At that same time, Ted Suss, Minnesota School Board Administrator, resigned and was replaced by Marsha Gronseth who believed the mascot changes were proving to be less painful than

AMBUSH THE INDIANS '89

TIGER HOMECOMING '89

Albert Lea
vs.
Owatonna

43

Slogan emphasizes reason for Indian mascot change

In football, teams are always pitted against each other. The other team is considered the rival. Opponents, as they are so aptly named, are opposed to each other. In choosing a Homecoming slogan then, it is only traditional to criticize the other team. Because the mascot represents the opponent's team as a whole, it is often the target of slogan language. But where does one draw the language line?

Our Student Council members unintentionally overstepped that line in choosing "Ambush the Indians." They should be commended, however, in their attempt to correct this mistake after several complaints were received.

For many teams, derogatory comments regarding their mascots are irrelevant because an animal or a fictional symbol cannot take offense. But in the case of the Indian, they can, and are, offended by derogatory slogans.

Becoming an issue during the past two years, many people have debated the use of an Indian school mascot. Those opposed to the mascot contend that its use creates negative racial stereotypes. Supporters of the Indian logo do not feel the change is necessary, citing that its use represents a positive image. The schools in question feel that they are honoring the Indian heritage, and it is the responsibility of their opponents to uphold their standards.

Earlier this year, the State Department of Education ruled on the issue, strongly suggesting that all schools using an Indian logo or mascot related to the Indian heritage choose a new one. Though no clear consequences exist if the mascots aren't changed, many schools have complied with the suggestion announced by Ruth Randall, commissioner of education.

Owatonna, our rival tonight, has not yet changed their mascot. The Tiger's slogan spotlights why a change is necessary. Although derogatory, the theme was chosen without awareness of the issues surrounding the use of American Indian names. The slogan had to be remade. In trying to make amends, the council subdued the slogan, using it limitedly. Floats for today's parade are barred from using the theme. Hall banners made promoting Homecoming are more compliant and we hope less degrading to the Indian heritage.

Less degrading, however, does not mean not insulting. Nearly any phrase used pummeling the Indians is a poor choice of words. When designing a Homecoming slogan, no school tries to be pleasant to the other team. Every phrase aims at destruction of the opponents. The decision to change traditional mascots is one to be upheld. Although Owatonna may not be acting discriminatorily against the American Indians, they should realize the burden being placed on their opponents and act accordingly, dropping the Indian mascot, or providing a viable alternative.

44

504 W. Clark St.
Albert Lea, MN
56007
19 September 1989

Mr. Alan Root
Principal/ALHS

Dear Mr. Root,

We, the members of the Albert Lea High School chapter of
Amnesty International would like to express our
unanimous opinion concerning the 1989 Homecoming
slogan. We feel that "Ambush the Indians" is
inappropriate. We feel that it is insensitive to their
contribution to our American culture and promotes old
stereotypes.

We realize that it is difficult to create or develop a slogan
concerning Indians when Owatonna retains their Indian
name.

We would appreciate anything you could do to change this
Homecoming slogan.

Thank you for your time and attention.

Sincerely,

Travis Allen Ausen
Amnesty International
Student Representative

Paul Goodnature
Amnesty International
Advisor

Cindy Johnson
Amnesty International
Member of Indian Heritage

students and administrators had anticipated. In December, 1989, the newly formed American Indian Advisory Committee[76] recommended to the State Board of Education that they ..." address the issue of the racist use of Indian mascots and logos in a broader context, beyond just urging that school districts eliminate the use of such logos". The Indian Advisory Committee asked that districts begin a discussion of "...what negative messages and themes are being taught through the use of Indian related symbols, emblems, and logos," and suggested that school districts establish Indian Parent Committees to help evaluate textbooks and a multicultural and gender-fair curriculum. This American Indian Advisory Committee also reaffirmed the May, 1988, resolution, encouraging school districts to eliminate the use of Indian logos and commended those school districts which had removed the logos, thus reaffirming the positions of St. John and CAIP and Stark and the MCLU.[77]

While school administrations were discussing these changes, the MCLU was continuing its search for a client. In order to speed up the search, Stark asked Willie Hardacker, another MCLU minority legal intern, to take on the difficult assignment of finding a client. That would mean traveling the state and meeting with Indian people who showed interest in becoming involved in the lawsuit. Armed with an affidavit which read "John Doe v. Minnesota School District Number ____ ", he set out with great hope that a client could be found somewhere in the state. The affidavit laid out the fact that using Indians as mascots is demeaning but also expressed fear of retaliation if the client's name was to become known. Stark also contacted Martin Farley, an American Indian and a chemical dependency counselor on the White Earth Indian Reservation, and asked him to join the search for someone willing to take that risk. Despite the contacts which Stark, Bellecourt, and Hardacker himself had made before leaving the Twin Cities for northern Minnesota, Hardacker found Indian people hesitant to sign on as a client. Most of those he spoke with on the White Earth and Leech Lake Indian Reservations agreed that using Indians as mascots was demeaning. But they also believed that by becoming a client or encouraging their school-age children to do so, they could be setting themselves up for ridicule and harassment from other Indians as well as from non-Indian neighbors.[78]

Chapter 7

ATLANTA BRAVES SHOWCASE RACISM WITH 'CHOP'

In a twist of sports fate, the Atlanta Braves and the Minnesota Twins faced off in the 1991 baseball World Series. At that time, sentiment against the use of Indian mascots and names was still extremely high among Indian groups in the Twin Cities. The American Indian Movement founders, Clyde and Vernon Bellecourt, were making plans for anti-mascot protests. On October 23, the *Star Tribune*, in preparation for the home games, printed an editorial called "Chopping away at insensitivity". It asked Atlanta fans to try to understand the pain their behavior causes American Indian people. Another editorial asked them to leave their tomahawks at home. "Congratulations and welcome, Atlanta Braves," it read. "But please, Georgians, leave your tomahawks, chants and headdresses at home. It's simply wrong to mock another people, to use their cultural symbols crudely, to resurrect hurtful old stereotypes...."[79]

By 1991, sentiment against the use of Indians as mascots had grown. Don Fraser, then mayor of Minneapolis, issued a statement of solidarity with the Indian people. United States Senator Paul Wellstone of Minnesota, and David Beaulieu, an Ojibway from White Earth, who was then Minnesota's Human Rights Commissioner, denounced the Atlanta team for its offensive behavior. Beaulieu said Atlanta's symbols "promotes racist ideas about American Indians." Matt Little of the Minneapolis NAACP and Gary Sudeth of the Minneapolis Urban League joined the chorus of support, as did the Minnesota Centro Cultural Chicano organization. Its director, Adam Acosta, compared the Atlanta Braves depictions of Indians to pictures of Mexicans sleeping under their sombreros.[80] The MCLU, CAIP, and the NCCJ were no longer alone. Now they were in the mainstream of the general public's attitude against the use of Indians as team mascots.

On opening day, hundreds of American Indians and their supporters gathered outside the Hubert H. Humphrey Metrodome in Minneapolis. Carrying signs that read, "I'm not a Mascot," "American Indians are not mascots for your fun and games," and the famous "Pennant Poster," protesters circled the stadium while thousands of Atlanta Braves fans carrying foam tomahawks booed their efforts. News reporters caught up with Jane Fonda outside the stadium to ask if she would stop doing the "chop". She agreed to refrain from it but before long cameras caught her doing an abbreviated version. As a flower child of the 60s and a former human rights activist, her behavior was deeply troubling to protesters who believed that she clearly understood its implications. Her husband, Ted Turner, the team's owner, simply refused to understand as he continued doing the "chop" accompanied by the eerie chant that mocked Indian people. AIM organizers, Clyde and Vernon Bellecourt, spoke to protesters and fans who would stop for a moment to hear their message. They too called upon Fonda and Turner to "stop the chop" and to change the name of their team. They were met by stony silence from both.

CBS sports spokesperson, Lou D'Ermilio, said he would listen to protesters so their position could accurately be represented on television. Valentin Obregon, a conciliator for the U.S. Justice Department's Midwest office in Chicago, also agreed to meet with people from the Atlanta team, the Twins, the City of Minneapolis, and Indian leaders to hear their concerns. He also planned to talk to fans and demonstrators outside the Metrodome. "I'm here," he said, "to determine how severe things are going to get...if we need to defuse a volatile situation." Braves third baseman Terry Pendleton thought the whole thing was much to do about nothing. "I wish they wouldn't take it personally," he said. "Basically, we're going out and having fun."[81]

The extensive media coverage of both the games and the protests gained the movement important visibility. Still, professional teams did nothing to change either their names or the mockery of American Indians that those names evoked. In fact, Fred Veilleux, a founding member of CAIP, was mocked when he attended game 5 of the World Series in Atlanta. He was carrying a sign that read, "American Indians are people, we are not mascots for America's fun and games. We deserve respect." In the book, *The Price we Pay: the case against racist speech, hate propaganda and pornography*, he described what happened to him there. "I was spit on. I was called 'chief' and 'Cochise'. Someone hit my sign with a toy tomahawk. People booed and jeered....They told me to get a job. As I walked through the city streets back to my hotel, the streets rang out with the sound of horns honking, Hollywood chants, and woo woo woo tomahawk chopping, and I had a feeling of loneliness in a city full of celebration," he recalled.[82] The next day Veilleux filed a complaint with the U. S. Department of Justice, claiming that his civil rights, under public accommodations laws, had been violated by the treatment he had received during the game in Atlanta.

Chapter 8

REDSKINS LOSE - RESPECT

A new year, 1992, brought some new players into the Indian mascot movement. Now newspapers, radio stations, and politicians began to take unprecedented, supportive stands. William Hilliard, editor of *The Oregonian*, announced he would no longer publish four team names: Redskins, Redmen, Braves, and Indians. Don Shelton, assistant sports editor at the *Seattle Times* announced that Redskins, Redmen and Red Raiders would no longer appear in headlines, photo captions, or quotes larger than the story. Radio stations, WTOP and WASH, in Washington D.C., stopped using offensive names when referring to American Indians.

And once again, American Indians and their supporters gathered in Minnesota to protest the AFL and NFL Super Bowl game where the Washington Redskins and the Buffalo Bills professional football teams squared off on January 23, 1992. Three thousand anti-mascot protesters spread out over six blocks in the icy weather on their way to the Hubert H. Humphrey Metrodome in downtown Minneapolis where the game was to be played. They circled the stadium, calling out their slogan, "Hey, hey, ho, ho, racist mascots got to go."[83] As they marched, onlookers and some fans taunted and cursed them across the police barricades. Washington Redskins fans, already decked in face paint and chicken feathers, jeered at the protesters.

But the comradery of the marchers could not be diminished by name-calling. Over 40 organizations or local chapters were represented - from the American Indian Movement, to the National Congress of American Indians, the National Association for the Advancement of Colored People, the Urban League, the National Organization of Women, the American Jewish Committee, United Auto Workers Local 879, and the United Church of Christ and the International Indian Treaty Council. It was a display of solidarity that happens only in times of intense social passion. "It was a day like no other, for me," recalls Pat Helmberger who carried one of the pennant posters. "I felt so close to all the other marchers even if I didn't know them. I was proud to be part of that movement."

In the last week of January, 1992, the National Coalition on Racism in Sports and the Media was born. It was the result of a two-day conference at Augsburg College in Minneapolis where civil rights leaders joined together to discuss on-going education of the public on the mascot issue. Matthew Little of the NAACP told the

group, "We give more and more lip service to the idea of multi-culturalism in America, and at the same time we can glorify and cheer the actual trashing of a people's culture."[84]

Charlene Teeters of the Spokane Nation told conferees of her experiences as an academically recruited graduate student at the University of Illinois where she was confronted with the racist antics of Chief Illiniwek, the team's mascot. "Everyone was wearing Chief Illiniwek paraphernalia on sheets, on their butts, on their cars, on diaper bags and on toilet paper," she said. "I came from a community that was very nurturing. I felt strong about who I was as a native person. To go to a place where they use this." She held up the roll of toilet paper. "No other race of people is used for a sports team identity. We are used as play things. That dehumanizes us. There is no question about it," she told the crowd at the Augsburg College conference.

Clyde Bellecourt reminded conference-goers that the use of Indian logos is a "multi-million dollar business," and if people do not understand the racism in the sports images, it would be hard for them to understand other issues facing Indian people, such as health care, education, water and treaty rights, and the concerns of Indian youth. Fred Veilleux, of CAIP, also spoke that day, warning Indian schools that by using an Indian name or mascot, they could be opening themselves up for racist behavior by opposing teams, in effect, perpetuating this form of discrimination.

On June 9, 1992, the Minnesota State Board of Education adopted a plan by staff member Dr. Will Antell to implement the policy already adopted by the board in its efforts to eliminate Indian mascots and sports team names. The plan consisted of five parts: 1) Develop a specific policy statement on eliminating racist and stereotypic treatment of American Indians. 2) Utilize the Inclusive Education Rule to eliminate racist and stereotypic treatment of American Indians within the entire school arena. 3) Generate support and cooperation from other education organizations. 4) Explore the potential for including an additional feature in contracts between schools for athletic competition which would prohibit the use of racist and stereotypic treatment of American Indians associated with logos and impose penalties for violation of the contract. 5) Use the monitoring and compliance authority of the Equal Education Opportunity Section in evaluating school districts regarding the use of racist and stereotypic treatment of American Indians.[85]

Yvonne Novak, a member of the Minnesota White Earth Chippewa Tribe and now the Manager of Indian Education for the Minnesota Department of Education, replaced Antell when he retired. She is in charge of monitoring the mascot issue and she stays in touch with the schools that have not yet changed. "We call them once a year to ask them if they are planning a change but we don't put pressure on them to do so," she said. She indicated that small towns are usually more emotional about changing team names. Many teachers in small communities were also students in those schools and have a deep attachment to the team name or mascot. "If the faculty doesn't see Indian caricatures as detrimental to self esteem, the kids are afraid to say anything. But when Indian kids have trouble staying in school, this (Indian mascots) doesn't help," she said.[86] Novak and other Indian people were pleased when St. Paul's Humboldt Public High School gave up its "Indians" name for a new hawk mascot. At a school ceremony retiring the old nickname, Indian drummers, dancers and singers added their voices to the students' farewell.

When the Burnsville school board finally voted unanimously in November of 1992 to begin its next school year with a new team name, St. John and Bellecourt were pleased.[87] "I think it's very big. A suburban team like that, a big team like that, will probably encourage others to do the same thing," said Bellecourt. St. John agreed although he admitted the decision had taken him by surprise. He had spoken to the students on several occasions and while he had always felt welcomed by them, he also felt that they wanted him to be sympathetic and understand that they meant no insult to Indian people. The *Star Tribune* in an editorial dated December 3, 1992, gave Burnsville an "A" on its decision, stating that schools that do not change should feel increasingly isolated.

Across the country in Washington D.C., Suzan Shown Harjo, director of the Morning Star Institute, a non-profit American Indian advocacy group, finally had had enough of the recalcitrant Jack Kent Cooke, owner of the Washington Redskins. She and other American Indians filed a lawsuit known as "Harjo v. Pro-Football, Inc.," with the Trademark Trial and Appeal Board in 1992. The lawsuit was directed at canceling the team's trademarks "Redskins, "Skins" and Redskinettes". Joined by other petitioners Raymond Apodaca, Vine Deloria, Jr, Norbert Hill, Jr., Mateo Romero, William Means, and Manley Begay, Jr., Harjo set out to demonstrate the long-term negative racial overtones of the Redskins name and antics. One of their exhibits was an advertisement for the Redskins/Giants game on

December 7, 1947. It reads, "Redskin Pow Wow... Redskin rooters have heap big time New York City Saturday Night. Sunday Redskin fans help Redskin Warriors Scalp Paleface Giants."

This lawsuit was based on the Lanham Act of 1946 which in essence says that a trademark shall be refused if it disparages persons or brings them into contempt or disrepute.(15 U.S.C. 1052(a)) The term "redskin" is defined in most dictionaries as a slang term considered disparaging and offensive. On April 2, 1999, the U.S. Patent and Trademark Office ruled that the name "Redskins" is disparaging to Native Americans, and the Washington team has no right to trademark such an insult. The ruling does not prevent the team from continuing to use the Redskins name and the related logos. But it could jeopardize the millions of dollars in revenue that the National Football League reaps from the sale of Redskins merchandise because the team would no longer be able to use federal law to prevent others from putting the logos on items such as T-shirts and caps.

Harjo, the lead plaintiff in the case, expressed delight in the decision."This is fabulous. I never expected to see justice done in my lifetime....This is an absolutely mighty landmark [of] societal change that we are watching."[88] The Washington team owners vow to challenge the ruling.

Altogether, five professional teams carry American Indian names/logos. They are: Chicago Blackhawks (ice hockey); Atlanta Braves (baseball); Cleveland Indians (baseball); Kansas City Chiefs (football) and Washington Red Skins (football). No professional team has ever changed its Indian name as a result of Indian protests but some colleges have done so.

Chapter 9

MORE SCHOOLS, THE *STAR TRIBUNE*, AND THE POSTER MAKE CHANGES

Public schools in Minnesota continued to make changes. Some used the opportunity as a teaching moment to help students understand the issue rather than simply making a change. Other schools were waiting for the MCLU to make another move on its threatened lawsuit, through lobbying or litigation. The civil liberties organization had not yet found a client for its lawsuit but few districts knew this. They did know, however, that the MCLU had a dogged determination to force the issue.[89]

Some movement activists were pleased when, in 1993, Brainerd High School decided to drop its logo which included an American Indian in a ceremonial headdress, but retain its Warriors nickname. Other activists believed that both logo and name should go. The school board, however, had unanimously approved the change even though the district's Indian Parent Committee had recommended that both the name and logo be replaced.[90] As of April 27, 1993, thirty-one public schools had replaced their Indian team names[91].

Fred Veilleux of CAIP stated in the May, 1993, edition of *The Circle*, "One of the reasons the remaining schools stopped short of changing their mascot names was that the President of the Minnesota Chippewa Tribe, Darrel "Chip" Wadena, stated publicly to the media, his criticism of the State Board of Education's resolution to eliminate Indian team names because the Board had not consulted tribal officials. Wadena who is also tribal chairman of the White Earth Reservation, stated further that the reservation tribal council passed a resolution supporting the Mahnomen school district in retaining its nickname the "Indians". Because of Wadena's political position, the public assumed he spoke for all Indian people."[92]

In 1994, United States Senator Ben Nighthorse Campbell from Colorado, introduced a bill that would prohibit the Washington Redskins football team from building a new stadium on federally controlled land unless owner Jack Kent Cooke agreed to change the team's name.[93] Cooke continued to refuse, saying "there was nothing in the world" wrong with using the 'Redskin' name and defiantly built his stadium on non-federal land in Virginia rather than in Washington D.C. St. John still wanted to encourage a change in the Indian names of professional teams. "If we could get black players to understand the issue, maybe they could push for change from within," he said. [94]

Also in 1994, the *Star Tribune*, in a move both ridiculed and praised in letters to the editor, made its own change from within when it told readers it would no longer use offensive Indian team names in their news and sports stories. Editor Tim McGuire and Julie Engebrecht, executive sports editor, explained that "repeated conversations with American Indians led us to appreciate the harmful effect of such nicknames....We have come to believe that discontinuing the use of these offensive nicknames is the right thing to do."[95]

On September 8, 1995, at the National Press Club in Washington, D.C., two days before the season opening for the Washington Redskin football team, a new poster was unveiled. NCCJ's Paul Sand, along with Tim Giago, editor of *Indian Country Today* newspaper, and Vernon Bellecourt, member of the National Coalition on Racism in Sports and the Media, were on hand for its unveiling. The poster, in vibrant red, yellow, and blue was designed to update the gray and black original. Mystic Lake Casino in Shakopee, Minnesota, owned by the Shakopee Mdewakanton Sioux Community, had funded the printing of this colorful poster that depicts fictitious pennants from the New York Fighting Jews, Chicago Blacks, San Antonio Latinos, San Francisco Orientals, St. Paul Caucasians, and the non-fiction Washington Redskins. The message was simple and direct: "Racism and Stereotyping Hurt All of Us. Native Americans Know This. Now You Do Too."[96]

With the poster as a vivid example, Paul Sand said, "The use of demeaning images of American Indian people as mascots and logos for sports teams is, and I repeat is, morally wrong. It denied respect they deserve as brothers and sisters. We must, as a multicultural society, oppose any use of ethnic or racial stereotyping. The time has come to put an end to this form of racism in our society." Michael Haney, a Seminole Indian from Oklahoma, and member of the National Coalition on Racism in Sports and Media, told the press that day that no one bats an eyelash at the use of the word "redskin" yet the "N" word in the O. J. Simpson trial evoked shock and rage across the nation and brought shame to detective Mark Fuhrman and the Los Angeles Police Department.

Racism and Stereotyping Hurt All of Us.
Native Americans Know This.
Now You Do Too.

Chapter 10

The Elements of Change in Minnesota

By February, 1996, thirty-eight of the fifty Minnesota public schools which had had Indian names/logos in 1988, had changed.[97] By May, 1998, only ten remained. It had been a long twelve years of turbulence and learning. Some of the changes had come about with little public discord. Other schools had made changes reluctantly. Some schools had merged and had decided that was the time to make a team name change. There were many other factors that made those changes possible in Minnesota.

First, there was an increasing number of American Indian people willing to speak up. Phil St. John, called by Ted Suss, "a voice crying in the wilderness," was one of the most significant. He helped Minnesotans - and Americans - understand the humiliation and anger that many Indian people feel when they see themselves portrayed as good luck symbols for sports teams. His power came from his willingness to be vulnerable; to speak about pain inflicted upon Indian children; to ask for understanding from those who had, for generations, inflicted the pain. "Perhaps this could be some kind of redemption for all the suffering of our grandparents," he said. "But being apologetic for racism is not enough. Enough is when white people make changes that enable our children to grow up in a world free of racism."[98]

Clyde and Vernon Bellecourt of the American Indian Movement were paramount in bringing the issue to the national stage during anti-mascot protests at professional sports events. Their skills at organizing and articulating the feelings of Indian people when they see themselves portrayed as mascots played a major role in public awareness. Their ability to draw elected officials and other human rights groups together during the protests helped the public understand that this was an issue of great importance despite the efforts of some to trivialize it. They also helped to bring the message to students in public schools, to administrators, and to school boards.

Then there was the MCLU with its leader, Matthew Stark, serving as the catalyst for public education and a legal confrontation. Stark, combative and determined in his battles for justice, never backs down when he believes the U.S. Constitution is on his side. His 'bulldog" reputation served the cause well as he went before the State Board of Education and television cameras to threaten a lawsuit against offending schools. And even though no client was ever found and no lawsuit ever filed, the effect of MCLU's lobbying, moral persuasion, and public education was undeniable. Ted Suss, former administrator of the Board of Education, believes that Stark and the MCLU were the major motivating factors in pushing for change. "That is their purpose for being and they have the legal style and expertise that this kind of issue requires," he said.[99]

The MCLU's role as the first non-Indian organization to publicly side with CAIP was significant and historical, too. No other American Civil Liberties Union affiliate, nor the national ACLU, played a role against the use of Indian mascots by public high schools during the late 1980s and early 1990s. It was not until 1994 that the Wisconsin Civil Liberties Union, as the second involved affiliate of the ACLU, adopted a similar position.[100] Interestingly, Ted Turner, owner of the Atlanta Braves, was elected in 1997 by the ACLU's national board to serve on the ACLU National Advisory Council. Stark, then a member of the ACLU's national board, publicly objected to Turner's nomination and election because of what Stark believed was his insensitivity to Indian feelings.

Then there were the public school personnel at many levels who listened to Indian people and came to believe that change was necessary and inevitable. Without an official mandate from the State Board of Education to school districts, but with a strongly worded resolution, they encouraged change and in nearly every instance, change took place. The process was often difficult but most non-Indian students in those schools came to understand that an Indian mascot or team name could hurt their fellow American Indian classmates and Indians in general. Dr. Will Antell, despite threats to his job security by an elected official, played a major role in shaping the policy that promoted such understanding. His gentle but unwavering pressure to put the policy into action was an important element in helping administrators, teachers, and students understand that Indian mascots promoted racism. Now only the most recalcitrant schools held on to their old mascots and names, stalwart in their belief that they honored American Indians. Without an official mandate from the state board, or threat of legal action, some of those schools may never change. Without the continued pressure from Drs. Antell and Stark, both of whom have retired from their professional positions, the mascot issue was over shadowed by other equally urgent concerns involving American Indians and civil liberties.

One cannot overlook the contribution of the Martin Williams Ad Agency in the creation of the pennant poster that became the trademark of the movement. The NCCJ, under the directorship of Paul Sand, played a vital role by distributing the pennant posters throughout the country. The simple message was undeniable: Indian people were hurt by the misuse of their images, names, cultures, and religions by sports teams. The only people who failed to understand the message were the owners of professional teams. And their explanations of "honoring Indian people" rang - and still ring - increasingly hollow.

A largely sympathetic local and national press gave encouragement to the cause. While some harsh criticism was directed, early on, toward Stark and the MCLU, by the *Star Tribune* and other smaller newspapers, that changed as more journalists came to understand the issue and the media's influence became significant in promoting the message of change. The *Star Tribune*, 5 years after questioning the MCLU's involvement in the issue, took a strong stand by eliminating the use of racist sports team names from their newspaper.

Minnesota's civil liberties and civil rights organizations and the Minnesota State Board of Education were first in the nation to launch a statewide campaign to end the misuse of Indian names and images by sports teams. It is a small but significant step in the ongoing process of justice but it is tempered by the knowledge that it was justice long denied and still too little implemented. Still, it is, for many involved in the struggle, a human rights issue of singular importance. As long as Indian people can be portrayed as mascots, as grinning or grimacing half-naked images waving scalps and carrying tomahawks or bows and arrows, there is no need to see them as real people with their own dreams and goals.

That is at the heart of this struggle - the recognition of Indian people as individuals, as parents, as community members, as children, as neighbors, as co-workers, as friends, and as citizens whose ties to this land precede by centuries the naming of America. Charlene Teeters of the Spokane Nation, left an important message with people who attended the 1992 conference of the National Coalition on Racism in Sports and the Media. She said, "To reduce the victims of genocide to a mascot or a stereotyped symbol is wrong, and it is just plain immoral. This is not a Native American issue. Don't sit around and wait for Native American people to tell you what to do. If you are an anti-racist, find out how you can challenge this in your community....Racism is never trivial, and it is the responsibility of all of us to address it."[101]

As this book goes to press, there are still a few public schools in

Star Tribune

Tuesday
January 25/1994

To our readers:

The Star Tribune soon will discontinue the use of certain offensive Indian team nicknames. We have not decided on the specifics of our new policy, and we were not ready to publicly announce the decision, but community conversation prompted us to do so.

Concerns have been expressed by American Indians about the use of such nicknames for several years. About two years ago, the Portland Oregonian decided to discontinue using the nicknames. At that time, we felt it was not appropriate for a newspaper to participate in a news event such as this one.

Since then, repeated conversations with American Indians led us to appreciate the harmful effect of such nicknames, prompting us to reconsider that decision.

We have come to believe that discontinuing the use of these offensive nicknames is the right thing to do. And we believe newspapers make decisions about language all the time. Many racist and sexist terms have been eliminated over the years.

The Star Tribune sports staff will be developing specific guidelines over the next week or so.

Tim J. McGuire
Editor

Julie Engebrecht
Executive Sports Editor

Minnesota which have not changed their Indian mascots or team names. Those schools are Benson (Braves), Isle (Indians), Mahnomen (Indians), Menahga (Braves), Red Lake (Warriors), Orr (Braves), Sleepy Eye (Indians), and Warroad (Warriors). The Red Lake school district is located on the Red Lake Indian Reservation, and is exempt from the name change resolution.

If you believe that the use of Indians as mascots in your school or community should be abolished, please do something about it. People, singly or together, who dare to take a firm stand against discrimination in any form, can make a difference for generations to come. That is one of the messages we hope this book will send to all.

Materials included in the Endnotes are in the Minnesota Civil Liberties Union files at the Minnesota History Center, Kellogg and John Ireland Blvd, St. Paul, Minnesota.

ENDNOTES

1. Data provided by Minnesota Department of Education, Indian Education Division, and refers to public schools only.
2. Data from Minnesota Department of Education, Indian Education.
3. Letters from Tracy J. Roel, Karen Skaja, and Steven Brenhaug were sent to the Sauk Rapids School Board members in August, 1986, complaining about the use of "Indian" as school team name and mascot.
4. 'Indians' team name is criticized," *St. Cloud Times*, August 28, 1986.
5. Interview of Steve Brenhaug by the author on September 8, 1998.
6. Memo from Sue Aasen to Debbie Mancheski dated December 1, 1986.
7. Letter dated September 15, 1986 signed by five members of the St. Paul Public Schools Multicultural Resource Center.
8. Interview of Steve Brenhaug by the author on September 8, 1998.
9. Appendix A.
10. Information from numerous interviews with Dr. Matthew Stark conducted by the author throughout 1997 and 1998.
11. The Northwest Area Foundation and The Otto Bremer Foundation.
12. Susan Aasen's resume.
13. MCLU Case File #I-6986.
14. Information from numerous conversations between the author and Phil St. John.
15. "What's in a nickname? Southwest's has a critic", by Mary Jane Smetanka, *Star Tribune*, April 27, 1987.
16. Pat Helmberger is a journalist and former member of the Bloomington, Minnesota Human Rights Commission. She also served as a member of the Intercultural Non-Sex Bias Committee of the Bloomington School Board. She is the author of this book.
17. The Concerned American Indian Parents was formed in 1987 by Phil St. John and other American Indians concerned about

the use of their images and names by sport teams.

18. "Southwest changes its nickname to Lakers", *Star Tribune*, May 30, 1987.
19. *Civil Rights Survey*, by Susan Aasen, November 24, 1987, is on file at the MCLU office in Minneapolis.
20. Charles R. Lawrence III, "The Id, the Ego, and Equal Protection: Reckoning with Unconscious Racism", *39 Stan. L. Rev. 317* (Jan. 1987).
21. Clyde Bellecourt is an Ojibway and one of the founders of the American Indian Movement.
22. Elaine Martin Salinas is an Ojibway and the former head of the Heart of the Earth Indian Survival School in Minneapolis. She is presently co-ordinator of Indian Affairs at the Minneapolis Urban Coalition.
23. Dr. Will Antell is an Ojibway Indian and was, in 1988, the State Director of Equal Educational Opportunities in the Minnesota Department of Education.
24. Ruth Meyers is an Ojibway from Duluth, Minnesota and, in 1988, a member of the State Board of Education.
25. Information from an interview of Dr. Matthew Stark by the author during 1997.
26. Interview of Ted Suss by the author on August 11, 1998.
27. Minnesota State Board of Education resolution dated May 9, 1988.
28. Interview of Dr. Will Antell by the author in 1994.
29. Interview of Jodi Cramsie conducted by the author on July 16, 1998.
30. "A politically incorrect World Series: Indians vs. Braves", *Minnesota Daily*, October 19, 1995.
31. A newspaper written by and for Indians in the Dakotas and throughout the country.
32. "A clever nickname cannot disguise a racial slur", *1988 Lakota Times*, by Tim Giago.
33. "Crimes Against Humanity", *Z Magazine*, pp.43-47, March 1993, by Ward Churchill.
34. Appendix B.
35. "8 Schools to keep Indian team name", April 4, 1989, *Pioneer Press*, by Nancy Livingston.
36. Interview of Dr. Will Antell by the author in July, 1999.
37. "Humboldt High rally backs Indian logo", *Star Tribune*, September 29, 1989, by Lydia Villalva Lijo. "Humboldt group wants Indian symbol", *St. Paul Pioneer Press*, September 25, 1989, by Nancy Livingston.

38. In an interview of Phil St. John conducted by the author on February 12, 1998.
39. 'Cottage Grove/Sioux tribe gives $10,000 to school that dropped 'Indians' nickname", *Star Tribune*, December 15, 1994, pg. 4B.
40. Minnesota Department of Education, Indian Education Division, data.
41. See Appendix C.
42. "ACLU on warpath over Indian nicknames", The Hibbing *Daily Tribune*, January 25, 1989.
43. "Commissioner urges end to Indian nicknames: Indian leader disagrees", *The Daily Journal*, International Falls, February 8, 1989.
44. *Detroit Lakes Tribune*, February 16, 1989.
45. Appendix D.
46. Appendix E.
47. "Sioux disappointed over names", *Waseca County News*, March 30, 1989.
48. "Why Indian team names should go", *Star Tribune*, April 23, 1989, by Jim Lenfestey.
49. *"What's in a Nickname?"* Franks, Ray; Ray Franks Publishing Ranch, Amarillo, Texas; 1982.
50. Ibid. Page 38.
51. Ibid. Page 114.
52. The Minnesota State Legislature moved to eliminate the word "squaw' from any lakes, ponds, or other geographical areas by the year 1996. Two American Indian students, Angelene Losh and Dawn Litzau, from Squaw Lake, Minnesota, began the campaign because the word "squaw" is offensive to Indian women. It is believed to be a French corruption of the Iroquois word "otsiskwa", meaning "female sexual parts".
53. Ibid. Page 97.
54. A story related to the author by Lakota George at a meeting in Shakopee, Minnesota, in 1992.
55. "Governor Edgar vetoes Chief bill", by Michael Dizon, *Daily Illini Online Archive* for 1995, July 17.
56. "Illinois Lawmakers Want U.S. Out of Mascot Controversy", by Dylan Rivera, *Chronicle of Higher Education*, Inc., July 21, 1995.
57. "Second letter suggests end to 'Redskin' mascot", *The Naperville Sun*, April 8, 1992.
58. An interview conducted with Professor Clara Sue Kidwell on July 20, 1998.

59. Letter from Clara Sue Kidwell to Dr. Matthew Stark, dated October 6, 1998.
60. *"Indians are us?: Culture & Genocide in Native North America,"* by Ward Churchill, Monroe, ME; Common Courage Press; 1994, Page 70.
61. *"Rooting for Who?"* by Jill Carlson, 1998.
62. Interview of Jodi Cramsie conducted by the author on July 16, 1998.
63. "Indians: A people, not a nickname", By Erik Brady, *USA Today*, August 15, 1988.
64. See Appendix F.
65. See Appendix G.
66. Information gathered from numerous interviews of Dr. Matthew Stark by the author in 1997 and 1998.
67. Copies of letters are on file at the Minnesota Historical Society, 345 Kellogg Blvd West, St. Paul, Minnesota 55102,
68. Copies of this report are on file at the Michigan Department of Civil Rights.
69. Interview of Arthur Stine conducted by the author on September 14, 1998.
70. Appendix H.
71. "Leech Lake band supports Indian team nicknames", by Larry Oakes, *Star Tribune*, March 23, 1989.
72. "Leech Lake band supports Indian team nicknames", *Star Tribune*, March 22,1989.
73. Information gathered from numerous interviews of Dr. Matthew Stark by the author in 1997 and 1998.
74. *Detroit Lakes Tribune*, page 8A, February 16, 1989.
75. Told to the author in separate interviews with Phil St. John and Dr. Matthew Stark.
76. The Minnesota legislature established the American Indian Advisory Committee in 1989. It was comprised of tribal representatives charged with advising the Minnesota State Board of Education on American Indian education issues.
77. See Appendix I.
78. An interview with Willie Hardacker on March 10, 1999.
79. "Leave the tomahawks in Atlanta", *Star Tribune*, October 19, 1991.
80. "More voices are raised against Braves' fans", by Randy Furst, *Star Tribune*, October 19, 1991.
81. "Toy Tomahawks, gestures by Atlanta Fans are called demeaning", *Star Tribune*, October 19, 1991.

82. *The Price we pay: the case against racist speech, hate propaganda and pornography*, edited by Lederer, Laura J. And Delgado, Richard; Hill and Wang, New York, 1995; pg 45-54.
83. "3,000 rally against racist mascots", by Eric Haase, printed in *The Circle*, February, 1992.
84. Ibid.
85. See Appendix J.
86. Interview of Yvonne Novak by the author on July 21, 1998.
87. Interviews with Phil St. John and Clyde Bellecourt, conducted by the author in 1998.
88. "Redskins Are Denied Trademarks", *Washington Post*, by Brooke A. Masters, Saturday, April 3, 1999.
89. Author's summary of interviews with Ted Suss and other Minnesota education department staff during 1997-98.
90. "Warriors to stay, but logo will go", *Star Tribune*, April 14, 1993.
91. Date provided by the Minnesota Department of Education American Indian Education Division.
92. "Educational Institutions Promote Racist Attitudes", by Fred Veilleux, *The Circle*, May 1993, pg. 6.
93. The *Washington Post*, Sunday, November 6, 1994.
94. Interview with Phil St. John, July 28, 1998 conducted by the author.
95. "To Our Readers": by Tim J. McGuire, Editor and Julie Engebrecht, Executive Sports Editor; *Star Tribune*, January 25, 1994.
96. "All-American mascots", by Tim Giago, *Indian Country Today*, August 4, 1995.
97. Data provided by Minnesota Department of Education, Indian Education Division.
98. Interview with Phil St. John, July 28, 1998, conducted by the author.
99. Interview of Ted Suss, conducted by the author on August 11, 1998.
100. Letter from the American Civil Liberties Union of Wisconsin to Department of Public Instruction, Madison, Wisconsin, dated April 25, 1994.
101. "3,000 rally against racist mascots", by Eric Haase, *The Circle*, February, 1992.

APPENDIX

AMENDMENT
TO THE
CONSTITUTION OF THE
UNITED STATES
OF AMERICA

Amendment XIV.**

Section 1. All persons born or naturalized in the United States and subject to the jurisdiction thereof, are citizens of the United States and of the State wherein they reside. No State shall make or enforce any law which shall abridge the privileges or immunities of citizens of the United States; nor shall any State deprive any person of life, liberty, or property, without due process of law; nor deny to any person within its jurisdiction the equal protection of the laws.

**The Fourteenth Amendment was ratified July 9, 1868.

MINNEAPOLIS PARK & RECREATION BOARD
200 Grain Exchange - 400 South 4th Street
Minneapolis, Minnesota 55415-1400
612.661.4800   fax 612.661.4777

ETHNIC, RELIGIOUS OR RACIAL NAME OR SYMBOL POLICY

It shall be the policy of the Minneapolis Park and Recreation Board that no program, event or activity offered by the Minneapolis Park and Recreation Board will use any ethnic, religious or racial names or symbols which may in the opinion of those groups create or perpetuate stereotypes which distort or degrade such groups.

Programs whose express purpose is to explore and celebrate the positive special contribution of such groups will be exempt from this policy.

Adopted at the <u>April 13, 1988</u>

Special Board Meeting.

OPPENHEIMER WOLFF & DONNELLY

January 19, 1989

School Superintendent
Sauk Rapids District Office
P.O. box 520
Sauk Rapids, MN 56379

Dear Sir or Madam:

I write this letter as an attorney for the Minnesota Civil
Liberties Union with respect to the MCLU's deep concern
over the use of school mascots, nicknames, or emblems
which involve or depict the American Indian. It is my
understanding that your school district uses the American
Indian as a mascot.

Use of an Indian mascot develops and perpetuates racist
perceptions of Native American, particularly when mascots
are used in connection with athletic events where students
may dress like Indians, howl, give out war whoops and
use symbols, such as feathers and headdresses, which
have religious and cultural significance for Native
Americans. Indians are a race of people with a separate
culture and religion that must be respected. Indians should
not be used as substitutes for animal symbols. The simple
act of having an Indian as a mascot is, in itself,
demeaning.

The MCLU does not stand alone in its view of Indian
mascots. Numerous associations, including the Association
of American Indian Affairs, Inc., The American Indian Law
Center, The Indian Affairs Counsel and Concerned
American Indian Parents, support our position.
Additionally, as you are aware, the Minnesota State Board
of Education in May of 1988 adopted a resolution that
declares that all mascots, nicknames, or emblems
involving the American Indian are racially derogatory, and
which requested that all schools cease their use. Your
district's continued use of Indian mascots not only flies in
the face of this resolution, but also flaunts the Equal

Protection guarantees of the Constitution of the United States, federal and state civil rights acts, and public accommodation laws.

This result is particularly compelling and appalling, since the school district is not running a commercial business - it is educating students. it is responsible for many of the fundamental attitudes and biases that students carry with them throughout their lives. neither the constitution nor society would permit a school to use black, whites, Jews or other races as mascots. Likewise, the constitution protects American Indians.

The MCLU asks that you change your school's mascot. In considering the change, you should be aware that the MCLU is fully prepared to, and will initiate suit against school districts which continue to use Indian mascots, asking the court to declare that the use of Indian mascots violates the federal and state constitutions, as well as civil rights and public accommodation laws. In such a lawsuit the MCLU will represent not only individual students, but also members of the Indian community who are damaged by the perpetuation of racial stereotypes; Indians who, in order to attend school athletic events, are subjected to watching their religious and cultural customs being degraded; and Indian rights groups.

We hope that you will step back and view this issue with clarity and arrive at the decision that continuing a tradition of using a certain mascot is not as important as ending the perpetuation of racial stereotypes that mascots foster in the school and community. Please let me know your decision at your earliest convenience. Thank you for your consideration.

Very truly yours,

Lucinda E. Jesson

cc: Bob Hicks

March 14, 1989

Ms. Barbara Nelson, Editor
Anishinabe Dee-Bah-Gee-Mo-Win
Box 478
White Earth, MN 56591

Dear Editor:

The following is in response to the article in the March
edition of the tribal newspaper titled, "Area people
perturbed about MCLU's letters of reprimand". I have
strong feelings about this statement because it infers
that the MCLU initiated this action against Minnesota
education institutions. I would like to take some of
your time to clarify this.

On March 20, 1988, my family witnessed a racist and
stereotypical event at a basketball game in the city of
Minneapolis. At that time, I felt it was time to try to
make some changes. After numerous meetings with
appropriate individuals in the educations system, I was
able to convince these people to make changes by
passing resolutions. The Minneapolis Public Schools,
the Minneapolis Park and Recreation Board and
Minnesota State Board of Education passed resolutions
in regards to our concerns.

At that time, we also formed the group that is now
known as the Concerned American Indian Parents. One
of our members worked for the MCLU at that time and
felt the same concerns that we had. Incidently, all of
our members are American Indians. With this
individual's expertise in legal matters, we were able to
put together letters and appropriate correspondence to
educational officials. On May 10, 1988, we went before
the State Board of Education with a resolution
demanding that all high schools in the state of
Minnesota that use American Indians as
mascots/namesakes, change or face the possibility of a

lawsuit. The resolution also stated that some schools might be exempted from this resolution if the usage was culturally and ethnically appropriate such as Red Lake High School and the Fond du Lac Ojibway High School. Although we have some reservations in regards to this, if appropriate mandated resolutions are included, we should be able to work this concern.

Therefore, this shows that the MCLU did not initiate this action but it was the efforts of the Concerned American Indian Parents that asked for changes. Your tribal chairman, Mr. Wadena, stated that they were not initially informed of this concern. I find that very hard to believe because we sent letters seeking support to every institution and selected individuals throughout the country. If I am not mistaken, Mr. Wadena personally received three letters. One addressed to the White Earth reservation, one to the Chairman of Minnesota Chippewa Tribe and one to himself because of his status as an American Indian leader. As for Mr. Christofferson, to state that he is joined by Mr. Wadena and not wanting to change, I find this hard to believe because again we have a white man giving us his views and trying to make decisions for the American Indian. It is amazing for me to hear that a man of Mr. Wadena's stature, is not aware of demeaning and derogatory racism that has been created by this type of stereotypical behavior. This presents a picture of a person that is caught between two cultures, one of which he has lost sight of and the other of which he is not a full member.

I would like for the people of White Earth to understand that this issue goes beyond the mascot issue. It includes housing, employment, educations, social and medical concerns of the American Indians. We cannot allow the white majority to continue to freeze us in time, we have to be allowed to progress along with the right to preserve our culture. We cannot allow the white man to continue to label us with his/her definition. We are not the screaming, wild west savage that Hollywood continues to portray. White people continue to label us and they say they are honoring us through respect. Again, it is their definition. We are not and never were the warrior, brave or Indian lurking on the ridge, waiting to attack innocent white settlers moving westward. We are survivalists. We were and still are, protectors of our families. Why doesn't the white man tell the whole story? Thanksgiving. Tell the whole story. If we do not make some positive changes now, our children will have to confront the same hardships that we had to confront. If certain American Indian adults do not see this as a problem, then they ought to move over; our efforts are not for them, but for our children. If you feel it is honorable for the white majority of Mahnomen to call their high school, Indians, I feel sorry because that is the only thing they are willing to share with you. Mahnomen is no different than any other white town located on an Indian reservation. There is so much racism, both overt and covert, that it might be hard to detect. Read between the lines. Thank you very much for your time.

In closing, try to understand my hurt and pain that my family has had to confront because of this type of negative behavior. There are many, many American Indian families throughout this country suffering from similar forms of racism. Please, try to understand our pain and hurt. Thank you.

Sincerely,

Phil St. John
Concern American Indian Parents

Indian mascots in schools violate Indian civil rights

The Minnesota Civil Liberties Union (MCLU) is continuing its support of Indian efforts to remove Indian names and similar designations from athletic teams in public schools throughout Minnesota.

A mascot is a person, animal or object adopted by a group as a symbolic figure believed to bring good luck. To characterize Indians as mascots for public-school athletic teams not only denigrates their culture, religious traditions and ethnic heritage, but is inherently dehumanizing.

Using Indians and their symbols as mascots sends the message that Indians will continue to be treated as less than full participants in contemporary society.

That this message is being sent via the state's public-school system, which educates youth and teaches the values of this society is even more opprobrious.

A public-school district, using public funds and public employees in a setting of compulsory school attendance, cannot dictate the name of its athletic teams by using the name of a particular group – be it Indians, redskins, Jews, Irish, Catholics, Turks, Japs, Nazis or Negroes – without violating the equal protection clause of the 14th Amendment of the U.S. Constitution.

The Minnesota State Board of Education has urged that the practice of using Indian names be stopped. Those efforts, as well as the efforts of the MCLU, are supported by the Minneapolis division of the National Conference of Christians and Jews, the St. Paul branch of the NAACP with the blessing of the national NAACP, the Minnesota Chapter of the National Association of Human Rights Workers and the Minneapolis Department of Civil Rights.

Also supporting the elimination of Indian mascots from public schools are the Association on American Indian Affairs, the All

National Indian United Church of Christ, the Minneapolis American Indian Center, the National Congress of American Indians, the Concerned American Indian Parents and many others.

Minnesota is not alone in confronting this issue. In October 1988, the Michigan Civil Rights Commission adopted a report concerning the use of Indian names and mascots by sports teams in Michigan educational institutions. The report said, "You will observe that the commission's position is that all use of Indian names and symbols should be eliminated."

Some individual Indians and Indian organizations, exercising their free-speech rights, disagree with the MCLU's position. However, we do not conduct popularity contests in determining our positions.

Eliminating racism, long-held stereotypes and biased attitudes often cannot be accomplished by mere reasoned dialogue. In fact, litigation and the threat of litigation has always been a strong force in changing people's attitudes and modifying their behavior.

Civil rights for minorities are never won easily in a society controlled by a dominant majority. If they were, the long and tragic history of the black civil-rights movement from the Civil War era until the present would have been written differently.

As for the MCLU not standing on principle, as the Star Tribune asserted in a March 26 editorial: Standing on principle is precisely what the MCLU is doing in this case.

What may have appeared to be the shifting sands of public perception and minority sensibilities during the years of the black civil-rights movement, the women's movement from the suffragettes to the present, the internment of the Japanese-Americans during World War II, the rights of the disabled and others, are now firmly part of established principle.

Being at the forefront when rights are violated, before they become "popular" and when there is risk, is what the MCLU has stood for in the past and continues to stand for today.

Matthew Stark, Minneapolis, Associate Executive Director, Minnesota Civil Liberties Union.

Independent School District No. 38
Red Lake Indian Reservation
Redlake, Minnesota, 56671

RESOLUTION

RED LAKE WARRIORS

WHEREAS: Red Lake High School does not have a school mascot; and

WHEREAS: "Red Lake Warriors" is the team name for Red Lake high School's football, basketball, baseball, softball, golf and other teams of high school competitive sports; and

WHEREAS: the tribal members of the Red Lake Band of Chippewas are themselves, American Indians; and

WHEREAS: American Indians have the right to select "Warrior" a term designating social status of previous and present heritage and culture; and

WHEREAS: "Warrior" in and of itself does not designate ethnicity.

THEREFORE BE IT RESOLVED that the Red Lake Board of Education petitions the State Board of Education to exclude the Red Lake High School Warriors from the State Board's resolution regarding mascots and petitions the Minnesota Civil Liberties Union to drop Red Lake High School Warriors from their suit.

Judy Roy   Dorothy Cobenais
Chairman of the Board   Clerk of the Board
Independent School   Independent School
District No. 38   District No. 38

March 3, 1989

Mr. Robert Hicks
Minnesota Civil Liberties Union
1021 West Broadway
Minneapolis, MN 55411

Dear Mr. Hicks,

Our group, the Concerned American Indian Parents, sincerely appreciates the support the Minnesota Civil Liberties Union has expressed relative to our concerns about demeaning and negative stereotyping of American Indians. The MCLU has stood with us from our initial confrontation with the Minneapolis Public School System and Southwest High School. We felt that the only resolution to the concern would have to be through legal channels and the MCLU has been gracious enough to provide us with this legal assistance. We look forward to working with this fine organization and continue to collaborate toward other related concerns. Our organizational goal is to have a national elimination of negative stereotyping of American Indians and with the assistance of the MCLU, we feel that we can attain this long range goal.

Sincerely,

Phil St. John

Phil St. John
Concerned American Indian Parent

PRESS 3/4/89

NICK COLEMAN

'Warriors' and Sibley don't mesh

Like other districts in Minnesota, the West St. Paul school district has reacted indignantly to the suggestion that the use of Indian team names reflects an anti-Indian prejudice.

Last week, the board of Independent School District 197 pronounced itself innocent of any stereotyping. The board voted unanimously to retain the nickname "Warriors" for the athletic teams of Henry Sibley High School.

Fine and dandy. If Warriors is important to the students and alumni of Sibley High, let them keep the nickname. But only if they agree to drop the name Sibley.

No matter where you stand on the issue of Indian nicknames, the combination of Warriors with the name Henry Hastings Sibley is terribly unfortunate. Sibley was to Minnesota's Indians what Simon Legree was to slaves. No one would dream of naming a high school team the Simon Legree Slaves, but

Henry Sibley Warriors is just as offensive.

Born in Detroit in 1811, Sibley was an America Fur Co. agent who arrived at the junction of the Mississippi and Minnesota rivers in 1834. The Dakota, or Sioux, Indians called it Mendota, meaning a place where two rivers join. Sibley built the first stone house in Minnesota. He also built a career that made him one of the wealthiest men in the state, and he did it on the backs of the Dakota people.

Sibley was Minnesota's first governor. For 31 years, he served on the University of Minnesota Board of Regents. he was the first president of the Minnesota Historical Society. That's the Henry Sibley who is honored by having a school (and a county) named for him. But that isn't his whole story.

Henry Sibley needs to be remembered today for something else. He should be remembered for the ruthless manner in which he

Coleman

exploited the Dakota people of Minnesota and for his actions that helped lead to the theft of Indian land and the near genocidal destruction of Minnesota's original citizens.

Sibley and Alexander Ramsey were instrumental in getting the Dakota to sign treaties in 1851 by which they gave up their land. The two founding fathers of Minnesota used lies, threats and bribes to coerce Indian leaders to sign treaties. Historians have called the process "a monstrous conspiracy."

One historian, Gary Clayton Anderson, has written that Sibley and Ramsey siphoned off scores of thousands of dollars in government money that was meant for the Indians. Sibley, for instance, paid himself a $35,000 "handling fee" for distributing treaty funds to other traders. In an era when the average man earned $200 a year, Sibley was rich – filthy rich.

The treaties forced the Dakota to live on a narrow reservation along the Minnesota River near New Ulm and led to starvation, disease and war. In 1862, the angry Dakota struck against white settlers, killing more than 500. Ramsey, who had succeeded Sibley as governor, named his old pal to lead white soldiers in a campaign of retribution against the Dakota.

On Dec. 26, 1862, 38 Dakota "Warriors" were hanged in Mankato by Sibley's men. Hundreds more were sent to prison. The surviving Dakota were expelled from Minnesota and endured years of hardship on arid land along the Missouri River. In 1863, Sibley led an expedition into what is now North Dakota, killing Indians who had nothing to do with events in Minnesota.

Honoring Henry Sibley's name with a high school might simply be more evidence that we are ignorant of our past and its meaning. But coupling his name with the nickname "Warriors" makes a mockery of any argument that Indian nicknames show respect for Native American traditions.

Dr. Bruce Anderson, super-intendent of West St. Paul schools, assures me the district is "very careful to hold in esteem any reference to Native Americans." He says the district plans to "review anything and everything to make sure that nothing exists that would be defamatory, derogatory or insulting to Native Americans."

Well, Dr. Anderson, let me make a suggestion about where you can start your review. Start with the name combination in your high school.

If you really want to honor Native Americans, you could consider changing your school's name to Dakota High School (your district, after all, is in Dakota County). Maybe you can come up with something better. But please, let's get rid of the Sibley Warriors.

Together, those two words make a painful combination.

Minnesota State Board of Education

705 Capitol Square Building, 550 Cedar Street, St. Paul, MN 55101 (612) 297-1925

DATE: March 1, 1990

TO: School District Superintendents

FROM: Minnesota State Board of Education

SUBJECT: STATE BOARD POSITION ON INDIAN LOGOS
AND   MASCOTS

The State Board adopted a policy regarding American
Indian logos and mascots at its February 13, 1990
meeting. A copy of the recently adopted policy is
attached, along with the related policy and implementation recommendations made to the Board by the
American Indian Advisory Committee and adopted by
the Board at its February meeting.

As the policy indicates, the State Board has not
rescinded its resolution that was adopted in May,
1988, urging school districts to eliminate the use of
American Indian logos and mascots. However, the
board believes that the scope of the issue should be
broadened to also focus on other curriculum areas.
Therefore, the newly adopted attached policy reaffirms
the board's action taken in 1988, as well as
incorporates the policy recommendations made in
recent months by the board's American Indian
Advisory Committee.

If you have further questions regarding this matter,
please contact the State Board's Executive Director,
Marsha Gronseth, at (612) 297-1925.

MG:ah:3948

Attachments

Minnesota State Board of Education

714 Capitol Square Building, 550 Cedar Street, St. Paul, MN 55101
OFFICE: (612) 297-1925 • FAX: (612) 297-7201

STATE BOARD OF EDUCATION POLICY ON AMERICAN INDIAN LOGOS/MASCOTS

The State Board of Education adopted a resolution in May 1988, which encouraged school districts to eliminate the use of American Indian mascots, logos and symbols. This resolution was based on the assumption that the use of such mascots and logos by the public education system often perpetuated negative racial stereotypes of the American Indian.

The legislature established an American Indian Advisory Committee in 1989. This advisory committee, comprised of tribal representatives, was charged with advising the State Board of Education on American Indian education issues.

In December 1989, the American Indian Advisory Committee made recommendations to the state board, in which they suggested that the board address the issue of the racist use of Indian mascots and logos in a broader context, beyond just urging that school districts eliminate the use of such logos. Specifically, the advisory committee recommended that the issue be refocused to address the racist and stereotypic messages and themes that are being conveyed and taught not only through the use of American Indian logos and mascots, but also in the curriculum.

In January, 1990, the state board received a draft of suggestions for addressing and implementing the policy proposed by the Advisory Committee in December. The suggestions include: 1) developing a policy statement on racist and stereotypic treatment of American Indians; 2) utilizing the multi-cultural and gender-fair curriculum rule to eliminate and stereotypic treatment of American Indians in the entire educational context; 3) generating support and cooperation from other educational organizations, such as the Minnesota High School League; 4) developing an additional feature in the contracts for inter-scholastic athletic competition which addresses the use of racist and stereotypic treatment of American Indians associated with logos; and 5) incorporating the monitoring and compliance responsibilities of the MDE's Equal Education Opportunity Section into the evaluation of school districts regarding the use of racist and stereotypic treatment of American Indians. The American Indian Advisory Committee has adopted these recommendations.

After reconsideration of this issue based on the recommendations made by the American Advisory Indian Advisory Committee in recent months, the state board adopts the following policy statement relating to the use of American Indian logos, mascots and emblems in the public education system:

"The State Board of Education reaffirms its resolution adopted in May, 1988, which encourages school districts to eliminate the use of such logos, and commends those school districts which have removed the logos from their schools. For example, emblems and mascots such as "Redskins" or "Redmen" must be eliminated from use by public schools. However, the state board recognizes that its resolution is not a rule, and therefore does not have the full force and effect of law. The state board also recognizes that some school districts have not removed their American Indian mascots and logos. Therefore, in order to assure that racist and stereotypic treatment of American Indians is eliminated and that school districts convey positive, accurate and non-racist images in all aspects of the school district curriculum and programs, the State Board of Education adopts the attached policy and recommendations made by the board's American Indian Advisory Committee regarding Indian logos, emblems and mascots."

The state board further directs the board and department staff to make any necessary technical changes to the policy and implementation recommendations made by the American Indian Advisory Committee and adopted by the board.

Adopted by the Minnesota State Board of Education: 2-13-90

POLICY RECOMMENDATIONS OF THE AMERICAN INDIAN EDUCATION COMMITTEE REGARDING INDIAN RELATED LOGOS

The 'Mascot' issue may be too narrowly defined. To eliminate all references to Indians in school logos, symbols and emblems does not necessarily solve the issue of negative and racist images in textbooks or those presented by teachers or non-Indian classmates, etc. Also, to eliminate all references to Indians without consideration of the themes and messages actually being conveyed has the potential of affecting the ability and willingness of schools and school districts to discuss anything about Indians in a multicultural curriculum.

The issue of Indian mascots should be broadened to also focus on the issue of what negative messages and themes are being taught through the use of Indian related symbols, emblems and logos. School districts and schools should convey positive, accurate, non-racist images in all aspects of the school district programs and curriculum including logos.

The State Board recommends that school districts with established Indian Parent Committees follow the provisions of the State Indian Education Act of 1988 regarding the role of Indian parents and parent committees in school district planning, including evaluation of the themes and images portrayed by logos.

The State Board recommends that school districts without Indian Parent Committees undergo an outside assessment of the images portrayed by their Indian logos as well as in the curriculum textbooks, etc., in order to eliminate all racist images of American Indians from the entire school arena including logos. A school district which refuses to actively change the negative symbolic contexts or themes conveyed by an American Indian logo should remove the logo altogether.

In implementing the Multicultural and Gender-Fair curriculum rule, school districts should not only seek the inclusion of positive information and knowledge about American Indians, but also the exclusion of stereotypical and racist references. Expanding the focus of the logo issue in this way should compel school districts to review and reform the entire school arena.

The State Board also recommends that the American Indian Advisory Committee develop a policy statement regarding racist and stereotypic images of American Indians portrayed in public schools.

Adopted by the Minnesota State Board of Education: 2-13-90

MEANS OF IMPLEMENTING THE POLICY RECOMMENDATIONS OF THE AMERICAN INDIAN EDUCATION COMMITTEE REGARDING INDIAN LOGOS

1. Develop a policy statement on eliminating racist and stereotypic treatment of American Indians.

It is recommended that a subcommittee of the American Indian Advisory Committee be established to develop a policy statement on racist and stereotypic treatment of American Indians. Such a statement will guide the evaluation of all aspects of a school district's programs and curriculum as it affects images of American Indians, their societies and historical experience.

This subcommittee will seek input and advice from other individuals such as representatives from Concerned Indian Parents and representatives of Indian parents from Humboldt High School.

A significant amount of information already exists concerning the evaluation of curriculum and textbooks, including the work of a National Indian Education Association program, Project Media, and the work of the Indian Education Project Task Force of the Education Commission of the States. The criteria and standards developed for the evaluation of textbooks and curriculum by these groups should serve as a foundation for an effort to develop a policy statement.

2. Utilize the Multicultural and Gender-Fair Curriculum Rule to eliminate racist and stereotypic treatment of American Indians within the entire school arena.

Using the Multicultural and Gender-Fair Curriculum Rule would provide a basis for the elimination of racist and stereotypic treatment of American Indian within textbooks, curriculum, pep clubs and rallies, or the images portrayed by logos, emblems and symbols.

A school district which continues to promote racist and stereotypic treatment of American Indians through the use of inappropriate images associated with logos, emblems and symbols would be considered in violation of the requirement that school districts maintain an "inclusive educational program" just as much as a district which did not change its curriculum to reflect positively on American Indians.

The Multicultural and Gender-Fair Curriculum rule requires the establishment of a local plan. This plan should include recommendations on how a school district will address the images portrayed by an American Indian logo, as well as issues related to behavior and slogans associated with sports events, pep rallies, etc. The state department of education will monitor and evaluate a district's plan through required status reports. The plan should also include a clear and precise policy statement on eliminating racist and stereotypic treatment of American Indians.

In developing the plan for implementing the Multicultural and Gender-Fair Curriculum Rule a school district is required to involve the district's Indian Parent Advisory Committee. The Indian Education Act of 1988 requires that Indian parent committees develop recommendations to the local board of education on all aspects of the school district's programs in consultation with the district's Curriculum Advisory Committee.

In developing and implementing the Multicultural and Gender-Fair Curriculum, a school district should also identify literature, curriculum material, and resource people related to American Indians, and provide necessary inservice training of teachers as required by the rule.

3. Generate support and cooperation from other educational organizations.

The state department of education staff will explore potential roles that other organizations may play in eliminating racist and stereotypic treatment of Indians associated with high school athletics. For example, the Minnesota High School League has a new policy on sportsmanship which requires schools to emphasize positive aspects about their own teams and avoid focusing on negative aspects of another team. The League also has a multi-cultural rule for referees and coaches. Other organizations such as the Minnesota State Board of Teaching, Minnesota Education Association, Minnesota Federation of Teachers, Minnesota School Boards Association, Parent Teachers Association, etc. could also provide support in eliminating racist and stereotypic treatment of American Indians in all aspects of a school district's program.

4. Explore the potential for including an additional feature in contracts between schools for athletic competition which would prohibit the use of racist and stereotypic treatment of American Indians associated with logos and impose penalties for violation of the contract.

5. Use the monitoring and compliance authority of the Equal Education Opportunity Section in evaluating school districts regarding the use of racist and stereotypic treatment of American Indians.

The Equal Education Opportunity Section of MDE is responsible to evaluate procedures, policies and practices which tend to discriminate against individuals on the basis of race, sex or physical condition. When a district is found in noncompliance they are required to respond with a plan to rectify the situation. Districts would be required to change discriminatory practices such as allowing racist and stereotypic treatment of American Indians through pep clubs and rallies, etc., which were condoned by the school district.

Adopted by the Minnesota State Board of Education: 2-13-90

3. PLAN FOR IMPLEMENTATION OF CURRENT BOARD POLICY ON AMERICAN INDIAN LOGOS/MASCOTS:

Will Antell, MDE staff, presented his preliminary action plan to implement SBE's policy on American Indian logos/mascots and symbols.

TOM LINDQUIST MOVED THAT THE BOARD ADOPT THE FIVE PART PLAN AND TIMELINE FOR IMPLEMENTING THE POLICY ON AMERICAN INDIAN LOGOS, MASCOTS AND EMBLEMS AS SUMMARIZED BELOW:

1. **Develop a specific policy statement on eliminating racist and stereotypic treatment of American Indians.** Dr. Antell will ask the American Indian Advisory Committee to establish a subcommittee to develop a policy statement on eliminating the racist and stereotypic treatment of American Indians. The sub-committee shall begin meeting in July, 1992, and complete it task by September 1, 1992.

2. **Utilize the Inclusive Education Rule to eliminate racist and stereotypic treatment of American Indians within the entire school arena.** Dr. will Antell and the American Indian Advisory committee will work with Dr. Norena Hale to develop an action plan.

3. **Generate support and cooperation from other educational organizations.** Dr. Antell will set up a series of meetings between the State Board with various organizations for support and assistance in eliminating racist and stereotypic treatment of American Indians in all aspects of school districts' programs. The Department will need guidance from the State Board on guidelines for carrying out this assignment.

4. **Explore the potential for including an additional feature in contracts between schools for athletic competition which would prohibit the use of racist and stereotypic treatment of American Indians associated with logos and impose penalties for violation of the contract.** The State

Board of Education will meet with the State High School League to discuss recommendations, which will be concluded by September 1, 1992.

5. **Use the monitoring and compliance authority of the Equal Education Opportunity Section in evaluating school districts regarding the use of racist and stereotypic treatment of American Indians.** Will Antell and the American Indian Education Committee will work with Barb Troolin to develop an action plan with timelines for Board consideration at its August 1992 board meeting.

ALAN ZDON SECONDED, AND THE MOTION WAS UNANIMOUSLY CARRIED.

INDEX